MICHAEL JACKSON

THIS IS A CARLTON BOOK

Published in Great Britain in 2018 by
Carlton Books Limited
20 Mortimer Street
London W1T 3JW

A CIP catalogue for this book is available from the British Library.

Editorial Director: Roland Hall
Project Editor: Ross Hamilton
Design Manager: Russell Knowles
Design: James Pople
Picture Research: Steve Behan
Production: Yael Steinitz

ISBN 978-1-78739-108-6

Printed in Dubai

10 9 8 7 6 5 4 3 2 1

THE COMPLETE MICHAEL JACKSON

THE MAN, THE MUSIC, THE MOVES, THE MAGIC

CHRIS ROBERTS

CARLTON BOOKS

CONTENTS

INTRODUCTION

It won't stop: we can't ever get enough. Michael Joseph Jackson (1958–2009) was, for over four decades, one of the world's most popular, influential and ground-breaking entertainers. Yet, even after his tragic death, his legend continues to grow. The best-selling musical artist in history outside of Elvis and The Beatles, his status as a star of stars, the Peter Pan of the pantheon, resonates as indisputably as ever. He won countless world records, Grammys and other awards, and sold around 400 million records globally. He was the charismatic, enigmatic King of Pop, with a peerless performance energy, a unique, eccentric style and an intriguing and turbulent life story, who changed forever what was possible in concerts, on video, in fashion and on the dance floor, and sang like a sensual angel.

From his professional debut at just six years old as part of The Jackson 5 alongside his four brothers, through a solo career with Motown Records and becoming the dominant entertainment star of the eighties and onwards into a new century, he continually shifted the boundaries. Racial barriers were broken down and fans of fire-fuelled music were lifted up. He transformed pop's understanding of the potential scale and dramatic potential of live shows and promotional films. Jackson was vital to the rise of MTV, and the crucial crossover between genres of music. Innovative dance routines, from the Moonwalk to the Robot – covering most points between – rewired our reflexes. *Thriller*, with its fountain of funky hit singles such as 'Billie Jean' and 'Wanna Be Startin' Somethin'', became the best-selling album ever made, with estimated sales of over 66 million copies, while *Off The Wall*, *Bad* and *Dangerous*, among others, were also huge sellers. Behind the groove, many revered Michael for his philanthropy and charity work, while others were fascinated by his unknowable quality, the mythology that surrounded him.

His private life was shrouded in mystery, and became a fevered media obsession as his modified appearance, personal relationships and lifestyle quirks were endlessly discussed, debated and analysed. There were scandals and court cases, gossip and rumour. When he announced his comeback tour, This Is It, we anticipated a glorious, critic-slaying, redemptive flourish, but fate cruelly denied us that with his death in June 2009. Yet, the flame burns – in 2016, Jackson's posthumous earnings were the highest-recorded annual amount by any artist in entertainment history. It was evident that his mystique and music, as well as retaining the loyalty of lifelong fans, goes on capturing the imagination and devotion of new generations.

This book celebrates Michael Jackson's magic and recounts the story of a supremely gifted, unorthodox individual, tracing his rise from innocent boy in a hard-grafting showbiz family to his hot-stepping solo years on top of the music world – in short, the most famous human on the planet. We will look at his two marriages, his business moves, his craving for a real-life Neverland, and those classic, immortal albums and songs, recalling their making and momentum. When aged just 22, he said he was "more comfortable on stage than any other place in the world… I just light up. I'm here on Earth for a reason, and that's my job – to make people happy." He added, "It's hard to live in the real world, in my position…" Michael's was not a conventional life, or a conventional talent but, at its zenith, his star shone brighter than the sun. It shines on.

Previous pages A young, smiling Michael Jackson at home in 1971, in the early days of his stardom.

Opposite Striking a signature pose, Michael dazzles crowds in Bremen, in 1997.

Following pages On stage in 1988, Michael performs at the peak of his powers.

> **"He was the charismatic, enigmatic, King of Pop, with a peerless performance energy, a unique, eccentric style and an intriguing and turbulent life story.**

HIST

ORY

THE EARLY YEARS

From the very beginning, the life of the boy who would be King of Pop was a long way from ordinary. Michael Joseph Jackson was born on 29 August 1958, the seventh of nine children. The siblings were initially raised as Jehovah's Witnesses by parents Joseph and Katherine (née Scruse) Jackson in the small industrial suburban town of Gary, Indiana. Their working-class neighbourhood was thought of as downmarket; their home was a barely-big-enough two-bedroom clapboard house. There was little around to hint that one day the street would be renamed Jackson Boulevard.

Father, Joe, worked as a crane operator for a steel firm, having unsuccessfully tried his luck as both a singer-guitarist and, by contrast, a boxer. Katherine had her hands busy raising this large family of boys – Michael, Tito, Jackie, Jermaine, Marlon and Randy – and girls, Rebbie, La Toya and Janet. She'd sing them

Below Forever young: Johnny Jackson (no relation) on drums keeps the beat for an early-days Jackson 5 in the mid-60s. Michael is bottom right.

Right Trophy cabinet: (left to right) Michael, Marlon, Tito, Jermaine, Jackie with parents Joe and Katherine.

JACKSON 5 BLVD.
JACKSON 5 BLVD

folk songs, but Joe was definitely the stricter parent, with something of a hot temper on occasion. Michael would later tell Oprah Winfrey in a TV interview: "There's a lot about my past life, my adolescence and my father that makes me very sad." Yet it was Joe who drilled the boys in singing and dancing, his sense of perfectionism making them go over routines repeatedly until they were flawless. He was perhaps frustrated that his own rhythm and blues band, The Falcons, hadn't become stars, and was dead-set on his talented offspring going further.

Michael's mother fondly recalled Michael being born "with a funny-looking head, big brown eyes and long hands. He was special." He was dancing by the time he was just eighteen months old, she said, to the sounds and rhythms of the washing machine – an early indication that Michael heard aspects of music that others hadn't yet discovered. "There was something different about him," said Katherine. "You know how babies move uncoordinated? He never moved that way. I don't believe in reincarnation, but – he danced like he was an older person." "I was just singing in a baby voice, imitating sounds I'd hear," mused Michael. "I didn't know what the words meant, but the more I sang the better I got. And I always knew how to dance. I'd watch Marlon, because he was only a year older than me, so I could keep up with him."

He'd remember his mother's random acts of kindness to strangers. He recalled a hurt, bleeding man knocking on doors in the street early one morning. "Finally he banged on our door. Mother let him in at once." Yet as his father placed pressure on the boys for constant improvement, Michael did consciously feel he was missing out on some precious parts of childhood. During early, youthful recording sessions, he'd glimpse other kids playing across the street in the sun, and wonder what it would be like to be allowed to join in. He'd stare at them "in wonder. I couldn't imagine such freedom, such a carefree life. I'd wish more than anything for that kind of freedom... that I could walk away and be just like them."

He wanted "to build tree houses, have water-balloon fights and play hide-and-seek with friends. But fate had it otherwise." Years on, he added, "Performing and making music undoubtedly remain as some of my greatest joys, but when I was young I wanted... to be a typical little boy."

Left Joe Jackson drilled the boys in all-singing all-dancing lessons.

THE 1960s

Fate indeed had it otherwise. By 1965, young Michael, along with the not-much-older Marlon, had joined the initial line-up of The Jackson Brothers, begun by Jermaine, Jackie and Tito with two local musician friends. At first his role was tambourines and congas, but he wasn't to stay on the fringes for long. He'd already been listening to Sam Cooke, Jackie Wilson, Stevie Wonder and Diana Ross, and admiring James Brown's dance moves. After Katherine heard him singing particularly well as he made his bed one morning, she encouraged him to participate in a school concert. His Gary "debut", singing show tune 'Climb Every Mountain' at a recital at Garnett Elementary School, drew a standing ovation from his teachers and classmates. His father Joe swiftly promoted him, first to backing vocals, then to lead vocals alongside big brother Jermaine. Jackie, speaking to *Rolling Stone* magazine, recalled, "He was so energetic; even at five years old he was like a leader. We all saw that. And the audience ate it up." It's safe to say Joe's eyes lit up.

Michael has suggested that Joe was too tough, too eager. He'd induce nervousness in the boys as they rehearsed. He'd sit in a chair watching with a belt in his hands, and "if you didn't do it the right way, Dad would tear you up, really get you. There were times he'd come to see me and I'd start to be sick." On another occasion, Michael would muse on this from a different, more generous perspective: "He seemed intent above all else on making us a commercial success. He was a managerial genius and my brothers and I owe our professional success, in no small measure, to the forceful way he pushed us. Under his guidance, I couldn't miss a step." Then he added, poignantly, "But what I really wanted was a Dad."

Dad booked them into the Gary nightclub Mr. Lucky's, then took them on tour as a warm-up act

Above The Jackson 5: (left to right) Tito, Marlon (front), Jermaine, Michael and Jackie Jackson.

Opposite Michael was already "a leader" at five years old, said Jermaine.

across the mid-West, where they even performed in none-too-salubrious strip joints, paid only in tips thrown on stage. It was one of young Michael's tasks to rummage across the floor, picking up any coins they might have missed, shoving them in his pockets. This inauspicious phase passed quickly, and the brothers were soon gaining more dignified professional slots. Michael, who would unfailingly wow audiences with his precocious gifts, was allocated – before he'd turned eight - a showcase solo routine in the middle of the set. He'd transform from shy, quiet boy to a star-in-waiting revelling in the glow of the bright lights. 1965 saw the group sing the Temptations' Smokey Robinson-penned hit 'My Girl' to win a talent contest at Roosevelt High School. Tito was at this stage a driving force, insisting they enter such contests, and it was his school-orchestra teacher who suggested they tweak their name to The Jackson Five.

Graduation to the next level was imminent. One of the young Michael's teachers, Gladys Johnson, was to inform reporters, perhaps apocryphally, "When he was five years old and had difficulty with his arithmetic, he told one teacher, 'Oh I don't need to learn those numbers. My manager will count my money.'" He's also reported to have said, aged five, "I would like to be a great entertainer. I want peace for the world. And I'd like to own my own mansion one day." In order to achieve these dreams, he was – among other lessons – studying James Brown on TV. He later told Oprah, "I thought James Brown was a genius. I used to watch him on television as a boy and I used to get angry with the cameraman, because whenever he'd really start to dance they'd be on a close-up so I couldn't see his feet. I'd be shouting, 'Show him! Show him!' I'd watch and learn." One influential person who was watching Michael with interest was the Chicago DJ Don Cornelius, who'd created the supremely funky TV show *Soul Train*. On his first impressions of Jackson, he told *Time* magazine, "He's only four foot tall, and you're looking at a small person who can do anything he wants to onstage, with his voice or his feet. That level? You're talking about James Brown as

a performer; Aretha Franklin as a singer. Michael was like that as a kid. He could do it all, in one package."

Joe Jackson was keen to book the boys on to various talent shows, including the prestigious Regal Theater in Chicago, and the Apollo in New York's Harlem. Naturally, they won both. The Harlem venue was famous for its "amateur night" contests, and their success there in August 1967 brought them to the attention of singer Gladys Knight, who sent a demo tape to her label boss Berry Gordy Jr, at Motown Records. The Detroit-based label rejected the demo, however, so Joe had the boys sign a record deal with the local Steeltown label in the November, resulting in their first single release – 'Big Boy' and 'We Don't Have To Be Over 21 (To Fall In Love)' – in January 1968.

Nevertheless, Berry Gordy had not dismissed the Jackson Five out of hand, and the boys' parents were highly responsive to his overtures, not least because they thought, rationally, that a child star had a limited window of time in which to make it big.

Michael understood this himself, to a degree. He'd already been known to request reshoots of photographs to place himself at the front, pointing out that it was "business", not "a family portrait". The president of Steeltown Records has noted his "...savvy. He knew. Even then." A friend of the Jackson family once said, "Katherine knew Michael was the only way out of Gary, Indiana. She said, 'Michael is cute now, but he won't stay that way forever. Then what would we do? We've got to get a record contract now.'" Berry Gordy, though, had as much savvy as anyone in the game. He saw the Jackson boys' ages as a challenge as much as a gift. Having already signed one teenage boy in ("Little") Stevie Wonder, he was aware of the obstacles that child labour laws could pose: these were then much stricter than they are today. Yet he found their videotapes of their live shows nothing short of irresistible, and, in July 1968, he set up a full audition. They delivered the goods, of course, being confident and consummate performers, with a cover of James Brown's 'I Got The Feelin' ' a particular highlight. On the day they thought Gordy looked unimpressed, but he's said that he was in deep thought, wondering if Michael's dance moves were too mature when juxtaposed with his high, boyish voice, and pondering how he'd choose suitable material for this unique talent. He later described his initial reaction as one of disbelief at "this old man in a young kid's body". Nonetheless, he wasn't going to let this opportunity pass by. He offered the contract the Jacksons had hoped for, and after he'd bought them out from their Steeltown deal with little fuss, they signed to Motown on 26 July.

The boys and their father were moved out to California, and set to work in Motown's famed Hitsville USA studio in 1969. Michael and Marlon, to their amazement, found themselves staying as house guests of Diana Ross, in her opulent mansion; the beginning of a long-lasting Michael–Diana friendship, wherein he never fully got over his awe at her presence. Acclimatizing as best they could, the boys kept up their work ethic, rehearsing diligently. Motown tweaked their name from The Jackson Five to The Jackson 5, which was better for graphics, artwork and logos, and started the press machine running. They fed journalists lines that suggested Michael was eight years old (instead of eleven), as well as the popular myth that Diana had single-handedly discovered them. Rehearsals were lengthy and gruelling. Perfectionism was still the goal; every song, part, routine and wardrobe choice was honed. Motown's styling team, The Corporation, planned the boys' path to stardom. It would have been a pressurized situation for any hopeful, rising performer, never mind one so very young.

Michael wrote, years later, "When I look back on my childhood, it is not an idyllic landscape of memories." He was to tell Oprah Winfrey, "It was lonely – having to think about popularity and all that. There were some great times with my brothers, pillow fights and things, but I did cry from loneliness. I was very little." Another telling quote he gave added, "I grew up in a fishbowl." Choreographer Vince Paterson said, "He's a little afraid of people. When people, from the time you're a little kid, want a part of you, your clothes, your hair – you're going to get a little nervous around people."

Yet fame was the aim and it was time for the boys to make their entrance into the public arena. This was done with some style. Diana Ross formally introduced them, like dancing debutantes, to 350 invited guests at the Beverly Hills Daisy Club on 11 August. They were soon lighting up TV shows, performing their debut single 'I Want You Back' for the first time on 7 October. By January 1970, it was number one, and their bizarrely titled debut album, *Diana Ross Presents The Jackson 5* swiftly sold a million. The seventies had arrived, and so had The Jackson 5. Michael was a star in motion.

Previous page Life's a beach: the young Jacksons pre-empt *Chariots of Fire*.

Right Mellow yellow: The Jackson 5 point the way to fame.

Following Page Skyriders: the boys show off their new bikes outside the new Encino, California house, bought for $250,000.

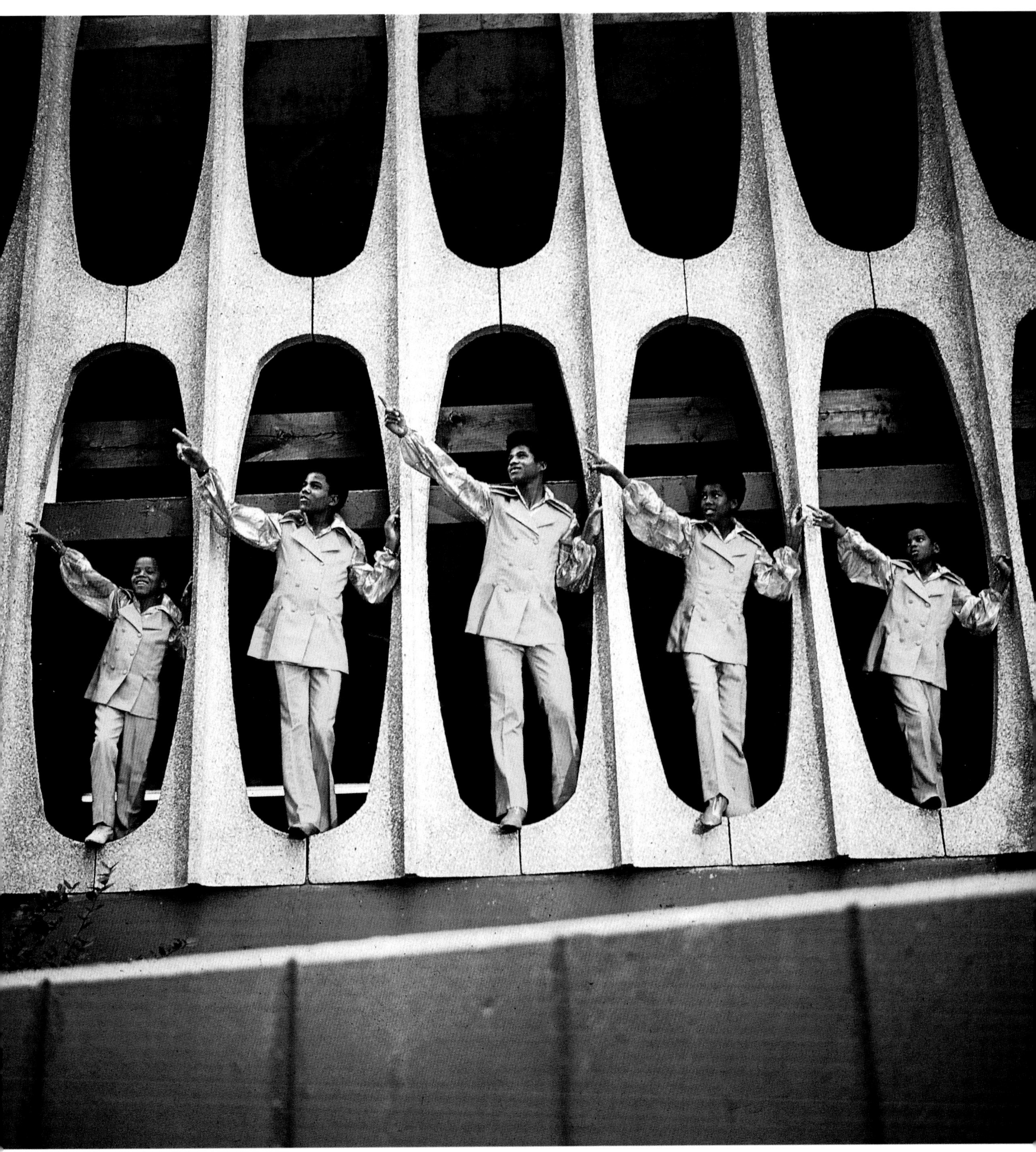

“It was lonely – having to think about popularity and all that. There were some great times with my brothers, pillow fights and things, but I did cry from loneliness. I was very little.

THE 1970s

It's sometimes overlooked now that The Jackson 5 had one of the most successful first years in pop history. They landed no fewer than four US chart-topping singles in 1970: no other band had previously got to number one with each of their first four releases, and no other Motown act had enjoyed four number ones in any one year. After 'I Want You Back' swept all before it, 'ABC', 'The Love You Save' and the clever change of tempo to a ballad, 'I'll Be There', did the same. Their album sat proudly in the Top Five.

Each of these four singles still stands tall as a pop classic. 'I Want You Back' gave the world its first gasp at Michael's vocal fluidity. The call-and-response interactions between the brothers zinged over rapid-fire rhythms, and Michael's voice skipped on top, his sigh of "ooh baby, give me one more chance" wooing radio listeners. 'ABC', released in February, was similarly flush with energy and catchy charm (it deposed The Beatles' 'Let It Be' from the top spot), and May's 'The Love You Save' kept up the magic and momentum. By August, it was time to draw breath, and the range of Michael's vocals was superbly showcased by the emotive 'I'll Be There'. He could sing a love song of such epic yearning, and he was only twelve. He later admitted that, in "honest to God truth", he didn't really know what he was doing: "I just did it. I never knew HOW I sang, I didn't really control it. It just formed itself." Some called it bubblegum soul, but when we listen to these tracks today, the soul has outlived the bubblegum. Author David Ritz got it right when he described this matchless opening flurry of hits as "moments of incandescent beauty, young and wildly optimistic – they make us happy." A phrase heard even more often than bubblegum soul was "Jacksonmania", which swept the United States. (And could be content with a less show-stopping, but very respectable, quartet of top ten hits in the UK, the four first releases peaking at numbers 2, 8, 7 and 4 respectively).

The success also meant that Michael's mother and sisters were able to join the family's menfolk in California. Reunited, the Jacksons moved into

Below Signed to Motown, the 5 enjoyed a run of hits.

Right Michael mastered the thoughtful pose early in his career.

Hayvenhurst, a sizeable gated mansion in Los Angeles. Their working schedule was relentless, but they did now have a family home in which to relax together – on the rare occasions they got a break.

We mustn't underestimate the part Motown played in their success, and similarly the boost the boys gave to the label, which was now branded as "The Sound of Young America". After Gordy had set up the label in Detroit in 1959, initially as Tamla Records, Motown's blend of songwriting had rejuvinated African-American pop, promoted racial integration, and brought black music from the underground into the mainstream. Artists as great as Marvin Gaye, Stevie Wonder, Diana Ross and The Supremes, Smokey Robinson, The Four Tops and The Temptations were rewriting the pages of the Great American Songbook. Thus, as the seventies settled into their stride, Michael Jackson became perhaps the first black superstar of the post-civil-rights era, in a radically different climate to the America of only a decade earlier. Black groups now appeared frequently on TV. The Chicago-raised writer Bonnie Greer has stated, "I understood viscerally the way The Jackson 5 dressed, what they referenced in their music and dancing. They belonged to me, to us, from the same background. Michael's family wasn't rich, except in prodigious talent and work ethic. You could latch on to Michael, because he was an African-American, because he was a black kid from a rough, blue-collar steel town."

Importantly, The Jackson 5 appealed to all ages, but Motown primarily targeted the younger generation. Tie-in merchandize from posters to patches promoted them as pin-ups, and there was an animated cartoon series, *The Jackson 5ive*, featuring fictitious adventures, fun and frolics, which received a large audience on Saturday-morning TV. Michael also appeared on Diana Ross's TV shows, showing a knack for comedy when – at a deliberately incongruous age – spoofing Frank Sinatra's 'It Was A Very Good Year'. Soon the brothers appeared in their own TV specials, *Goin' Back To Indiana* and *The Jackson 5 Show*. They were mobbed if they walked down a street, although this wasn't something they got to do very often even if they wanted to, as Gordy had their diary bursting with travel, concerts, TV appearances and recording sessions. Plenty of recording sessions. In the six years between 1969 and 1975, they recorded, incredibly, no fewer than fourteen albums. And that's before you even factor in Michael's solo releases. One can only imagine the stresses this placed the boys under, especially for young Michael, under. It's been reported that he had to pretend to be asleep

Opposite The Jackson 5's stage wear grew increasingly flamboyant.

Above One of the world's most photographed people, behind the camera.

when his older brothers were bringing girls back to hotel rooms on the road, and that even as his fame rocketed he was fretting about ordinary growing traumas like acne, his self-image not being able to keep pace with his public one.

Europe was soon to catch full Jacksonmania. October 1972 saw the band's first tour of the continent, including a Royal Variety Command Performance at London's Palladium theatre, plus shows at the Wembley Empire Pool (now Wembley Arena), and a triumphant appearance on the major UK TV music show *Top of the Pops*. They enjoyed being tourists, sight-seeing at the likes of Buckingham Palace. A concert review in *The Times* moaned about high ticket prices, but observed presciently, "Fourteen-year-old Michael has an astonishing command of gesture… His twinkling feet scarcely seemed to touch the stage." Meanwhile, the hits kept coming, quantity with quality: 1970 gave us 'Mama's Pearl', 1971 'Never Can Say Goodbye', 1972 offered 'Lookin' Through The Windows' and 'Doctor My Eyes' (a Jackson Browne song), while the following year, 1973, emitted 'Hallelujah Day' and the almost psychedelic 'Skywriter'. Great as most of this material was, its thunder was arguably stolen somewhat by the onward march of Michael's solo career. Initially perceived by Gordy as a profitable double-your-money sideline, it was already developing a drive and flair of its own. His albums *Got To Be There* and *Ben*, both released in 1972, were too successful on both aesthetic and commercial levels to be anybody's idea of an afterthought.

The lovely 'Got To Be There' had been Michael's solo single debut in 1971, which the 13-year-old had sung with even more passion than on 1970's 'I'll Be There'. The public thought so too, taking it to number four in the US (and number five in the UK). Gordy and Joseph Jackson were increasingly keen to push his solo status, but at first Michael thought the notion of performing without the familiarity and comfort zone of his brothers would be intimidating. While The Jackson 5 were still a big machine, it was Michael's face which adorned most teenage bedroom walls, and Motown and Michael's father saw that his talent burnt the most brightly. Michael, too, with his offstage confidence growing, began to acknowledge it. Gordy commented on his intensity. As Michael racked up further classic solo hits like 'Rockin' Robin' and his timeless reading of Bill Withers's 'Ain't No Sunshine', those in and around the inner circle could feel a shift coming. When the single 'Ben' went to number one, the mood was confirmed, even though this Oscar-nominated song (tied in to a horror movie) about a slightly creepy friendship with a pet rat – which Donny Osmond had passed on – was an unorthodox pop smash. It possibly seemed less odd to Michael, who famously loved animals, and was already bringing strange pets such as peacocks, parrots and a boa constrictor into the family home. A hint of things to come.

Momentously, Michael's voice was breaking, its sound thus crucially changing, and big decisions had to be made. He struggled with puberty – it "messed up my whole personality," he later confessed – and disliked the inevitable changes to his appearance it naturally brought. He didn't feel sufficiently ready or secure or emboldened to leave The Jackson 5 at this point, despite singing 'Ben' solo at the 1973 Academy Awards. In a surprising plot twist, however, the group wanted to leave Motown. The ahead-of-its-time 1973 album *G.I.T.: Get It Together* and number-two hit single 'Dancing Machine' had shown they were keen to glide away from simple pop-soul and tackle more funky, disco-leaning rhythms. Yet, Berry Gordy was keen on caution. As the brothers' stardom had accelerated, friction had developed between the Jackson parents and the Motown boss. The Jacksons decided they needed and deserved more creative control than the micro-managing Gordy was allowing them, and of course there were disagreements over money. So, in 1975 the group as an entity parted company with the label.

'Dancing Machine' had proven a mighty catalyst for their new aims and direction, and introduced a prescient new Michael move. Of their red-hot performance of the track on *Soul Train*, *Time* magazine had written, "It was an altogether funkier Michael

Previous pages Michael's youthful vocal tones began to blossom.

Opposite Life on the road could be exhausting at times.

Above London calling – the Jacksons hit the Hammersmith Odeon.

Jackson doing the singing. Mid song, his face went blank as he popped through a jaw-dropping dance move called 'the Robot'. It was his own invention, the product of long hours of cunning physical engineering, nothing borrowed from James Brown." Whether Jackson had invented it or not, the "robot" soon caught on as a dance craze. Michael was, continued the review, "done being a prodigy and onto something bigger." Yet the split with Motown was complicated, not least because Jermaine Jackson – who had married Gordy's daughter Hazel – stayed with the label. Randy became a full member of the band, and after dropping the "5" and amending their name to The Jacksons for legal reasons, they signed to CBS Records, later aligning with their Epic Records branch. They updated their image and clothes and initially thrived with a stream of global hits, swinging effortlessly between genres, as if driven to prove a point to Gordy. Their 1976 debut album *The Jacksons* saw them working with revered Philadelphia writer-producers Kenny Gamble and Leon Huff, and the silky-smooth, slinky 'Show You The Way To Go' became a memorable British number one. That album also witnessed Michael's debut as a solo composer, with writing credits for 'Blues Away'. By 1978 the million-selling album *Destiny* was self-produced, and delivered enduring dance anthems like 'Blame It On The Boogie' and 'Shake Your Body (Down To The Ground)'. Michael was now a regular co-writer, his skills maturing fast, his innate understanding of groove and rhythm evident. There were further Jacksons successes ahead, such as 1980's *Triumph* and 1984's *Victory* (no title, apparently, could be too celebratory), but the latter was to include Michael's final full sessions with his brothers. No group was big enough, now, to contain his unique potential and presence. As he reached the age of 20, he was ready and eager to make an even

Previous pages Michael with younger sister Janet, a long time before they dreamed up "Scream" together...

Above One dove: Peace on Earth.

Right The Jackson 5 were stars of stage, TV and even a cartoon series.

Following page Michael's stage presence is undeniable in this photo from the Destiny tour at the Rainbow Theatre in London, 1979.

“ Michael’s skills were maturing fast, his innate understanding of rhythm and groove evident… no group was big enough now to contain his unique presence.

more indelible mark on music history. His brothers could only watch as he went up another gear. *Off The Wall*, his last album of the seventies but the first of a whole new era both for him and popular music, was one giant leap. He jumped from dazzling professional to stellar, maverick genius.

Going it alone wasn't a straightforward path overnight, however. In fact, one trip up a yellow brick road brought some early stumbles. His onscreen charisma had been obvious for years, and it wasn't a surprise that he was cast, aged 20, in the movie of *The Wiz*, an African-American musical reimaging of the classic *The Wizard Of Oz*. On Broadway, the show had been a smash. Now Michael was teamed up with old pal and mentor Diana Ross: he to play the Scarecrow, she Dorothy. Richard Pryor and Lena Horne were also given parts. Experienced, esteemed director Sidney Lumet took the helm, and Quincy Jones wrote the score and served as musical director. Everything was set up for a triumph.

Something didn't click, though. As Diana and Michael skipped and hopped from Kansas to a disco-fied New York, the very expensive movie flipped uncertainly between smart-ass quips and hallmark schmaltz. The songs, too, were substandard for such titans. For all Michael's athleticism and energy, *The Wiz* fizzled, and flopped. He personally enjoyed the experience – "I don't think it could have been any better" – and critics at least noted his "genuine acting talent". And the key thing that came from it, the seed that came to shape the eighties, was his meeting, and rapport with, Quincy Jones.

Jones was an already legendary producer who'd worked with Frank Sinatra, Ray Charles, Ella

“ When Quincy and I first started, we sat down and discussed exactly what we wanted – and it's all turned out just the way we planned.

Fitzgerald and Aretha Franklin. He and Michael got on well, an instantly cohesive blend of youthful enthusiasm and wise guidance. Jackson asked Jones to produce his next solo album, which he was referring to as his debut as "a grown man". Jones said, "He wasn't sure he could make it on his own. Me too, at first – I had my doubts." But any doubts were swiftly blown away. "When Quincy and I first started," said Michael later, "we sat down and discussed exactly what we wanted – and it's all turned out just the way we planned." Indeed, *Off The Wall* worked like a dream. It shaped the sounds, styles, rhythms and images which would propel Michael to the status of world's biggest star. Released in 1979, it effectively kick-started the eighties. It went eight times platinum, eventually sold twenty million copies, became the first solo album to yield four US top ten hits, including two chart-toppers, and made Michael a household name. The tuxedo and white socks he sported on the cover, became something of a visual catchphrase, a terpsichorean trademark. (His manager reckoned that the tuxedo was his idea, but that the socks were Michael's). Jackson was also now a frequent co-writer, though the lion's share of compositional credit went to the great late Rod Temperton (who'd studied Michael's vocal technique in depth beforehand), as well as starry names, such as Paul McCartney and Stevie Wonder. 'Don't Stop Til You Get Enough', 'Rock With You', 'Working Day And Night', 'She's Out Of My Life' and the title track are of course now established as shimmering, vibrant landmarks on the map of pop culture.

It wasn't all a groove. While *Off The Wall* was going off the hook, Michael was experiencing more challenges in his offstage life. Family relationships continued to struggle under the strains of fame. When he turned 21, in August 1979, he fired his father, Joe Jackson, as manager. John Branca, an attorney, took his place, with Michael telling him his goal was to be the "biggest and wealthiest" star in the business, no less. Although *Off The Wall* was a sensation by any standards, he wanted more. He said it was "totally unfair that it didn't get Record of the Year, and that can never happen again." In truth, despite only winning one Grammy (for Best Male R&B Performance for 'Don't Stop...'), it won multiple other awards and was breaking records. Yet the singer was dissatisfied. "I wasn't too happy with the way it was accepted. I said, for the next album, I refuse to let them ignore me. I set my heart on it." A wide-eyed kid no longer, he was driven with a steely perfectionism. He'd even taken charge of the Encino family mansion, refurbishing and remodelling it in a kind of mock-Tudor fashion, and building in the grounds of the estate a down-scaled replica of Disneyland's Main Street USA. This being Michael, dozens of animals now roamed the grounds freely.

He'd also undergone an operation after breaking his nose during an overzealous dance routine. The surgery, however, wasn't entirely successful and he felt that subsequent breathing difficulties were hindering his vocal ability. More operations, and rhinoplasty, followed. This was the unfortunate beginning of a lifelong near-addiction to such procedures, as the desire for perfection pushed led down a regrettable road. And while his mother admitted concern about how quiet he'd become – "he said he feels like an animal in a cage" – Michael was telling the press that he was more comfortable on stage than in daily personal interactions. Asked by one interviewer if he'd ever one day retire from performing, he laughed, saying "No way! Don't stop 'til you get enough!"

He was always unabashedly positive about the joys of dancing, a form of escape from reality. "When dancing," he wrote poetically, "I felt touched by something sacred. In those moments, I felt my spirit soar and become one with everything that exists. I became the stars and the moon; I became the lover and the loved." Said one admiring professional dancer, more practically, "It's the combinations which really distinguish him as an artist. Spin, stop, pull up leg, pull jacket open, turn, freeze. And the glide where he steps forward while pushing back. Spinning three times and popping on his toes. That's a

Left Growing up: The Jacksons continued but Michael, now 20, was cutting loose solo.

Next page, left *Off The Wall* capped off an exciting period of transition for Michael.

Next page, right Michael dances with his 21-year-old sister La Toya in an apartment they shared on the East Side

trademark move that a lot of professionals wouldn't try. If you go wrong, you can really hurt yourself."

Michael was somewhat hurt when the magazine *Rolling Stone*, as he perceived the turn of events, turned down his offer of a cover story. His pride stung, he discerned an element of racism. "I've been told over and over that black people on the cover of magazines don't sell copies. Just wait. Someday those magazines are going to be begging me for an interview." He added with a glint of mischief, "Maybe I'll give them one. And maybe I won't."

If these tales suggest contradictions and paradoxes, Michael was full of them. He, as an enigma, was just getting started. His friend, the film mogul Steven Spielberg, once said, "I've never seen anybody like Michael. He's an emotional child star, yet in full control. Sometimes he appears to be wavering on the fringes of the twilight, but there is a great conscious forethought behind everything he does. He's very smart about his career and the choices he makes. I think he is definitely a man of two personalities."

If *Off The Wall* had been the icing on the cake of the seventies, Jackson was now keen to see what lay behind that wall if you knocked it down; to know where the eighties would take him and where he would take them. He was over that wall now; in another zone. He and Quincy Jones were to make magic together for another nine years. His radical reboots and reinventions – both of his music and his image – were gathering momentum. He was adamant that his next phase of work would be an absolute planet-conquering monster. Thrillingly, it was.

Left On the Destiny tour, Michael's destiny seemed to be solo stardom.

Above Fans go wild for their favourite funkateer.

Next page Lapping it up – Michael soaks up the Jacksonmania.

THE 1980s

I knew we could do anything," said Michael as he experienced the epochal *Thriller* era of his career. "Its success transformed many of my dreams into reality."

When he and Quincy Jones and their team reconvened at the Los Angeles studio where much of *Off The Wall* had been hammered out – Westlake Audio Studio A, Beverly Boulevard – they had lofty ambitions, but even they didn't know that what they were about to produce would come to define a decade. With Michael established as a grown-up R&B star, *Off The Wall* having proven his chops beyond doubt, he was hungry to go further. (As a mark of his status, even an old reissue like 'One Day In Your Life' had raced to the top of the UK charts in June 1981, but his voice and music had since moved on apace.) His pride meant that he felt *Off The Wall* could have done more, even if few others thought so. The increasing fame meant added media intrusion, a knock-on effect that he didn't enjoy. His family links too, were becoming cloudy. Michael was less than pleased with his father's priorities and dealings. The more Joe Jackson tried to bring him back into the family camp, the more he pursued outside bonds regarding his management and business interests. The central point was that he wanted to be bigger than he believed his father's management skills could make him. He wanted to be not one of the biggest, but *the* biggest.

To this end, he wanted to make an album where every song was a potential hit single. It had to be "three times as great" as *Off The Wall*, and he'd take his time "and get it right. I'm a perfectionist. I strive. I'll work until I drop." Quincy Jones tried to temper his cravings, suggesting that the record-buying market was volatile and you couldn't predict anything. Together they sifted through hundreds of songs to find the finest, debating long and hard over their choices. (Famously, they even disagreed at first over the extended bass line intro to 'Billie Jean'.) Yet, Jones got caught up in Jackson's fever, and studio engineer Bruce Swedien said, "I've never seen Quincy more into anything, ever. On the first day, he told us, 'OK guys, we're here to save the recording industry.'" In turn, Jones, a man who in more recent times has shown he loves a dramatic quote, said of Jackson, "It was like he was going to make it this time or die trying."

Incredibly, the masterpiece was recorded in under three months, and was released on 30 November 1982. It was number one on the *Billboard* chart by February 1983 and stayed in the charts for no less than 37 weeks, often making return visits to the top spot. It was on its way to being exactly what Michael had envisaged – the biggest-selling album of all time. It wasn't uncommon for the album, which won a then-unmatched eight Grammys, to shift a million a week. A stunning seven of its tracks were US Top Ten hits, with 'Billie Jean' and 'Beat It' both number ones. Over the next four years, Michael earned over 700 million dollars. He had become the titan of music and show business he'd dreamt himself into being. "In *Thriller*," wrote the *Village Voice*, "Jackson has begun to part the shimmering curtain of his innocence – it's magic, it's unreal – to glimpse darker, deeper things. Once that curtain is ripped down, the view could be astonishing."

While we'll examine the album itself in more detail elsewhere, the impact of *Thriller* on both the man himself and pop culture at large must be discussed here. This was his imperial phase, where he was introducing the Moonwalk, revolutionising the art form of the video, and even meeting President Ronald Reagan at the White House.

Before 'Billie Jean', MTV was almost exclusively devoted to white acts. Michael broke that barrier down, and made the video the most powerful tool in getting your music across to a wide, unsegregated audience. Said Tommy Mottola, later head of Sony Music, "He totally defined the video age. Nobody before or after Michael could do what he did for video. He put the MTV culture into the forefront." It's hard to overstate the impact back then of the electricity in his footsteps on 'Billie Jean', the *West Side Story*-style gang fights of 'Beat It' and of course the werewolf horror tropes of the 14-minute video for 'Thriller'. The last was by far the most expensive video ever made at that time, coming in at close to a million dollars. Directed by John Landis, who'd made one of Michael's favourite films, *An American Werewolf in London*, it grew from the seed of the singer asking of the director, "I want to turn into a monster – can I do that?" Once that possibility was established, Michael insisted on hiring Landis (at great expense) for the job, as well as make-up pioneer Rick Baker. "With Michael, business is bigness," said one industry insider. "Every new venture has to be bigger than Disneyland." The video had a premiere screening, being a bigger event than most full movies. Diana Ross and Warren Beatty were among the attendees. Landis described it as "incredible". There was a standing ovation; shouts from the star-studded audience for an encore. Landis explained there wasn't anything else to show; that was it. "So show the goddam thing again!" hollered Eddie Murphy. This they did.

Right The *Thriller* era begins: "I knew we could do anything."

It's surprising perhaps that Michael didn't instantly embark on a huge world tour to promote and capitalize on the triumphs of *Thriller*, but the videos, expensive as they were, were doing much of the promotional heavy lifting. Yet if anyone doubted his ability to produce magic onstage of which nobody else was capable, one night in March 1983 blew those doubts away. The NBC TV channel had arranged a 25th anniversary of Motown special, *Motown 25: Yesterday, Today, Forever* to be filmed at LA's Pasadena Civic Auditorium. What happened that night served to confirm Michael Jackson as the world's most brilliant and talked-about pop star. He danced the planet to the moon and back.

Thriller was still sitting resplendently at number one when Michael was asked to perform a medley with his brothers at this event (a benefit for sickle-cell anaemia). As Berry Gordy had cleverly made it a charity concert, it was tough even for those artists who'd drifted away from him, often on frosty terms, to refuse. And Michael's arm was being twisted by emotional appeals from his brothers. A gigantic TV audience of 47 million watched as a reunited Diana Ross and The Supremes, Marvin Gaye, Stevie Wonder, The Four Tops, The Temptations and Martha Reeves and The Vandellas performed their flawless classics.

The Jacksons finished their collective medley with 'I'll Be There', but as the other brothers left the stage, Michael went into his own extra song routine for 'Billie Jean'. His starrier status, having outgrown the siblings, was thus acknowledged, but few can have anticipated how joyously he would seize the moment. Poetry in motion ensued as – in a blue sequinned jacket, one white glove, white socks visible under short black trousers – Michael took hold of a trilby. His lightning-fast moves and freezes were both spontaneous-seeming bursts of raw energy and deliciously, meticulously choreographed. All of the Motown stars and hierarchy knew they were witnessing something special. As for the television audience, they certainly weren't switching channels.

For a generation, the Moonwalk moment was their equivalent of The Beatles on *The Ed Sullivan Show* back in 1964. Now, technically, it – or an approximation thereof – had been done before. Greats of movement like Fred Astaire, Cab Calloway and Marcel Marceau had forged various illusions of floating backwards, and in 1982 Jeffrey Daniel of disco-soul group Shalamar had pulled it out of his locker on the UK TV show *Top of the Pops*, causing a hubbub of interest. Michael had seen Jeffrey do it on *Soul Train*, and some say he asked him to teach him the trick. Regardless, Jackson here not only nailed it but whisked it up into a breathtaking brand of magic. For viewers, it was a classic "Where were you when...?" moment. Even the lord of dance Astaire phoned him up the next day, congratulating him – and perhaps handing on the mantle – with the comment: "You're a hell of a mover, son. You really put them on their asses last night. You've got rage in your feet. I'm the same way." This compliment wasn't lost on Michael, who promptly visited his octogenarian idol in Beverly Hills and taught him some Moonwalk steps. He later dedicated his autobiography *Moonwalk* to him. Gene Kelly, too, joined in with the acclaim. School kids everywhere tried to copy the moves. (And all the while, sales of *Thriller* kept on leaping higher and higher).

The Moonwalk moment has gone down in pop history. As *Entertainment Weekly* roared, "A delicate young man with a choked voice, a white glove and magic shoes... took the microphone and began to write the next chapter of American music history. Squealing,

Opposite Hello, is it me you're looking for? A disguised Michael with Lionel Richie.

Above Michael peruses the *Thriller* press reviews.

> **On that hallowed ground, with the cream of black American music there, he performed 'Billie Jean' with the Moonwalk and it was gobsmackingly brilliant.**

moaning, spinning, taking the viewer's breath away... the music industry had to throw away its old yardstick of success."

Success was now Michael's bread and butter. The night of the Moonwalk at *Motown 25* boosted sales of the *Thriller* album again. His impact, however, was being felt around the world, and outside such limits as chart statistics. As the R&B star Akon later recalled, "Everyone wanted to be like him. He was a kind of god in Africa." Sir Bob Geldof happened to see Jackson do the Moonwalk at the Harlem Apollo that year, and said, "On that hallowed ground, with the cream of black American music there, he performed 'Billie Jean' with the Moonwalk and it was gobsmackingly brilliant. The place just went wild. A brilliant artist, a fantastic dancer."

As the game-changing duo of 'Billie Jean' and 'Beat It' were followed to number one in 1983 by the duet with Paul McCartney, 'Say Say Say', the 1984 Grammy Awards were all but a tribute to Jackson. His eight trophies – including one for Best Children's Album for his collaboration on Steven Spielberg's *E.T.* – broke a record of seven held since 1970 by Paul Simon in the year of *Bridge Over Troubled Water*. Michael revealed a new look for the ceremony, sporting military uniform and aviator shades, a self-invented style he was often to revisit. He took actress Brooke Shields and

Opposite A class act – Michael spruces up his image.

Below Jackson talks with CBS Records chairman Maurice Oberstein while in London to accept a gold disc for the The Jacksons *Triumph* album.

child actor Emmanuel Lewis as his guests, but denied rumours of a romance with Shields. He could perhaps have chosen his words more delicately. "I took her to help her out," he said, shrugging. "It was good PR for her to be seen with me." Brooke concurred that they were just friends and there was "no romance". Adding that he was "nice", she discussed the set-up later. "There were a handful of former child stars at the time. We were friends because we shared an understanding of how difficult life could be in the public eye." Lewis, for his part, declared, "Michael is the best friend you could ever have. He's gentle, not rough like other guys." This gentle man also won eight American Music Awards and three MTV Awards. All the acclaim he'd desired from *Off The Wall* had come to him now via *Thriller* and his accompanying charisma. 'Beat It' was used in a government campaign to discourage underage drinking, and so Michael was invited to the White House to receive another award, for services to the relevant charity. John Branca stated that Michael had "a lovely day", while the First Lady, Nancy Reagan, after praising his songs and their message for saving lives, was, strangely, less diplomatic. Of Michael she said: "So peculiar! A boy who looks just like a girl, and whispers when he speaks. He wears a glove on one hand, and sunglasses all the time. I didn't know what to make of it!"

If that was strange, Michael's response to being granted a star on the Hollywood Walk of Fame could be seen as even odder, as he attributed the honour to his pets. His pets, of course, were not those of the average everyday household. "I think nature and animals are very inspirational to my work. The majority of my success comes from that; I just play off it. I love animals." He listed his unorthodox private zoo: "I've got a llama, two deer, a sheep called Mister Ted and all kinds of birds and swans." He also had a snake named Muscles, who inspired the sublime hit he wrote for friend-mentor Diana Ross. If you're wondering why Bubbles, the chimpanzee, wasn't mentioned, Michael didn't adopt him until 1985. His eccentricities

Above *Off The Wall* was still winning multiple awards around the world.

Right Michael's evolving look proved confusing to First Lady Nancy Reagan.

Following pages *Time* magazine declared Michael "the biggest thing since The Beatles, the hottest phenomenon since Elvis".

l'amour

were played down by *Thriller* engineer Bruce Swedien. "OK, so he has some animals – we're ALL crazy about animals. OK, so he has had his nose changed a bit – that's just normal in LA."

In fact, the growing perceived eccentricity was becoming a part of the Jackson image, a factor in the global brand. At this stage it didn't overshadow the music, talent and natural star quality. More talked about was the way in which his appeal had created a crossover star equally adored by fans of every colour and nationality. Demographics merged in their enthusiasm. Today, we take as given the fact that white and black styles of music interact and interject with each other, but nobody before Jackson had entwined funk, soul and rock so fruitfully, or at least to such a degree of popularity. His dance moves were mimicked by all. He wasn't thought of as being of a particular ethnicity; he was seen chiefly as a boundary-collapsing, rare yet unifying superstar, the one and only Michael Jackson. *Time* declared him "the biggest thing since The Beatles. The hottest single phenomenon since Elvis Presley." Showing that they did acknowledge his roots, they added, "He may just be the most popular black singer ever."

Even at-their-peak superstars can have bad luck and calamities. Michael accepted a fat fee to shoot a Pepsi Cola commercial in LA, even though he refused to drink the product. His friend Paul McCartney advised against this move, suggesting it would cheapen his image to do something that could be perceived as tacky or money-grabbing. Michael may well have wished he'd listened to Macca when the advert's big budget on-set pyrotechnics leapt out of control and his hair was set alight. Fire extinguishers were rushed out and Michael was wrestled to the ground by rescuing helpers. The director of the advert, Bob Giraldi, who Michael knew from his shooting of the 'Beat It' video, had suddenly realized that Michael was trying to hurriedly tear his jacket off, fearful the fire had spread to his torso. He reckoned it wasn't such a huge deal, insisting, "It was over before it started." Yet the media went into spasms of hysterics, and some might say they never thereafter stopped. Michael was sent to hospital for a precautionary check-up, and on learning that there were banks of TV cameras and reporters outside, put on his one white glove to wave from his stretcher. His head was bandaged and in fact the incident had been genuinely painful and frightening. He'd suffered second degree burns, and some gossips

Left David Bowie, Bette Midler and Cher join the early 80s Jackson fan club backstage.

reported him having hair and scalp problems for years afterwards. His $15 million fee to endorse Pepsi for three years was perhaps more arduously earned than many had expected.

Jackson's management team, especially John Branca, were, however, generally hitting home runs. *Thriller* remained "the pulse of America" (*Time*, 1984) and Branca has claimed that he secured his artist a royalty rate (two dollars for every album sold) that was higher than any ever received in the business at that time. *The Making of Thriller*, an offshoot documentary funded by MTV, sold furiously. Then there was the merchandising – for example Michael Jackson dolls at $12 dollars a pop. Michael encouraged such ventures: he'd phone Branca almost every day, urging more and more promotion. When Thriller eventually fell to number two, it's said that he was close to tears. Yet

Left Michael and Brooke Shields, both former child stars, were rumoured to be dating but were "just good friends".

Below Say, say, say – when Macca and Michael were friends and collaborators.

Right I want Muscles – Michael's animal collection grew in size and strangeness.

> **Kid, the press will build you up today because they like to tear you down tomorrow...**

it had given the entire music industry a fresh shot of confidence, and Michael was hailed as "a one-man rescue team for the business. A songwriter who sets the beat for the decade. A dancer with the fanciest feet on the street. A singer who cuts across all boundaries of taste and style and colour too."

On 7 February 1984, *Thriller* made the *Guinness Book of World Records* as the world's best selling album. The Reverend Jesse Jackson praised what he saw as its wholesomeness: "No vulgar artist ever became so famous as Michael Jackson." Even Frank Sinatra wanted to meet him. The author Darwin Porter has written of the coming together of two generational icons, the older offering weathered advice to the younger. "Kid," said Sinatra, "the press will build you up today because they like to tear you down tomorrow. In show business, you're hot – and then oblivion. Very few entertainers can make a successful comeback – I'm the comeback kid. And frankly, I thought you were washed up in the seventies. Who would've predicted *Thriller*?" Jackson would have been impressed by Sinatra's staying power. He had a respect for most things old-school and Hollywood. He'd told the UK magazine *Smash Hits* – in a Christmas 1982 phone interview with Mark Ellen, the last British interview he gave – that he loved old MGM movies and screen stars like Katherine Hepburn (who he also befriended) and Spencer Tracy, as well as his pal Spielberg's *E. T.* "I mean," he said, "Who doesn't want to fly?" He said it was wrong to think he liked all horror movies just because of the 'Thriller' video; in fact he "couldn't sleep" if he watched one. Musically he expressed affection for The Beatles (especially 'Yesterday'), Simon and Garfunkel, Elton John and – perhaps admiring

Opposite "A dancer with the fanciest feet on the street."

Above Famous for much more than 15 minutes: Andy Warhol meets the Jackson gang.

their frontman's ability to rock a military jacket – Adam and The Ants. He confided that he still lived with his "folks" – albeit in a much bigger building than in younger days. "I'd die of loneliness if I moved out," he confessed poignantly. "Plus, I couldn't control the fans and stuff I'd be surrounded."

He soon made some new friends, whether it be in the form of a three-year-old chimpanzee or the planet's biggest singing stars as they warbled 'We Are The World'. Bubbles was rescued in 1985 from a Texas cancer-research facility and became the main man – well, monkey – in Michael's menagerie. Not exactly playing down the eccentric role, Jackson found a matching military jacket for Bubbles and took him along to parties and media events. He said he'd taught Bubbles to Moonwalk. Terrific publicity, at first, by Michael and his promotional team, but this is where the "weird" label began to balloon, and escalate worryingly. The lines between reality and fantasy started to blur. News outlets ran wild, spurred on by the undeniable changes in Jackson's appearance. The stories soared and scarred: he was sleeping in an oxygen tent, he wanted to buy the bones of Marilyn Monroe or the Elephant Man. Some of the tales were invented and bonkers, others bore a dash of truth. The nickname Wacko Jacko started to hog headlines.

There was no doubt that his skin was getting lighter. According to the star, this was because of a pigmentation disorder known as vitiligo. Newspapers nonetheless reported a "bleaching" process. Over the next few years, there were multiple appointments for plastic surgery, his nose becoming thinner and sharper, his eyelids lifted and his lips reduced in size.

Above The bejewelled white glove became one of Michael's iconic trademarks.

Right Michael's appearance was soon to change in surprising ways.

His chin, seemingly out of nowhere, developed a remarkable cleft. A face that had been so youthfully pretty was shape-shifting to become... extraordinary. Something was chipping away at Michael Jackson's exterior, and we can only speculate on the internal demons that nudged him to such choices.

In the mid-eighties though, spirits were high as success piled upon success and the Band Aid and Live Aid projects in Britain moved millions to music-inspired charitable donations. In January 1985, American artists made their own grand gesture with 'We Are The World'. Michael co-wrote the song with Lionel Richie, the pair putting it together within twelve hours of it being suggested. A grand line-up of US talent was assembled in LA, on the night of the American Music Awards, with stars recording both before and after the Hollywood ceremony. Even some who weren't conveniently there for the Awards decided this was something they couldn't and shouldn't miss out on. Michael himself, the top attraction, didn't get to the awards, as he was hurriedly prepping the chorus with Quincy Jones, again producing. It was one stellar cast list, with Stevie Wonder, Diana Ross, Paul Simon, Tina Turner, Bruce Springsteen, Billy Joel, Bob Dylan, Willie Nelson, Dionne Warwick, Kenny Rogers, Smokey Robinson and Bob "feed the world" Geldof involved, as well as several of Michael's siblings joining the chorus. A more than healthy range of styles and genres were thus represented, and maximum appeal ensured. Quincy, along with Harry Belafonte, had actively urged some of the stars to participate, sending a quick demo by Michael and Lionel around, recommending they all "check their egos at the door". Michael's stirring vocal entrance on the bridge of the sentimental song was arguably its high spot. Credited to USA For Africa, 'We Are The World' was a global number one, the enthusiasm of Michael and friends raising over $50 million dollars for the noble cause.

Another huge amount of money was involved when, later that year, Michael displayed again a canny eye for good business. This time he rather tarnished his friendship with Paul McCartney by doing so. When The Beatles' song catalogue and publishing rights became available for sale he outbid Macca and John Lennon's widow Yoko Ono, making him the owner of the ATV catalogue. (He'd also outbid the considerable financial muscle of Coca-Cola, Sony and Warner

Bros.). This brought him in around $7 million per year for several years, but McCartney felt offended and somewhat duped. "Our friendship suffered a bit of a blow." To him it felt as if his erstwhile friend – they'd paired up on 'Say, Say, Say' and 'The Girl Is Mine' as well as 'The Man' on Macca's *Pipes Of Peace* album – had both stolen his family jewels and ostentatiously asserted his status and wealth. When the unwitting Sir Paul received a phone call from a reporter, it was the first he'd heard of the purchase. Jackson now held control of every Beatles song written between 1964 and 1971. As he phrased it, "I've found the Holy Grail." A peeved music-industry executive remarked, "Despite that little girl voice and delicate manner, Jackson is one hard-nosed son of a bitch in business." That wasn't the end of it – Jackson also took out a multi-million dollar insurance policy on McCartney's life. "God," sighed McCartney, "he'll make millions when I'm gone." And when Michael allowed Beatles songs to be used in commercials, like the controversial deployment of 'Revolution' in a Nike advert, McCartney was close to losing his enduring bonhomie. He said Jackson had "trashed the reputation of The Beatles. He seemed so nice and polite when I met him. But he has a heart of gold – and I don't mean that as a compliment." This gold-digging side of Michael spurred him to instruct John Branca to also acquire the rights, too, to Sly and The Family Stone's releases, and records by Little Richard and Dion and The Belmonts.

Meanwhile the Jackson family were undergoing crises. Katherine, believing Joe to be cheating on her, filed for divorce. Joe was said to be splashing his children's earnings on his extra-marital affairs, yet he adamantly refused to leave the family's Encino mansion and the pair were caught up in labyrinthine legal tangles which showed no signs of being resolved promptly. One report claimed that Michael sighed sadly, "She'll never escape." He, however, was continuing to soar away from his roots, nurturing friendships instead with Hollywood icons such as Elizabeth Taylor and Ava Gardner and hanging out

Opposite Never one to miss a photo op., boxing promoter Don King poses with the Jacksons.

Above Michael and early mentor Diana Ross had fallen out but made up by the time of 'We Are The World'.

Following pages Dressing down: Michael in uncharacteristically understated wardrobe choice, prepping for the 'Bad' video.

LA MODA

with everyone from Marlon Brando and Robert De Niro to Andy Warhol and Jane Fonda. Brando joked that President Reagan would call Michael for advice on "how to run the planet".

For all these starry distractions and familial worries, Michael was determined not to lose the focus or momentum of his musical career. He set to work fashioning the follow-up to *Thriller*, a tough act to follow if ever there was one. Recording sessions took place between November 1986 and July 1987. And five years on from the release of *Thriller*, the big and bold *Bad* broke cover at the end of August. The publicity drive was worldwide, and naturally the album landed straight at the top of the *Billboard* chart, becoming the first ever to produce five number one singles. With Spielberg unavailable, Martin Scorsese, no less, directed the $2 million dollar video for the title track, with Michael revealing his new leather-and-chains bad-boy-biker image. *Bad* soon joined *Thriller* on the all-time best-sellers list. Michael as a crotch-grabbing quasi-punk startled some, but the attention it stirred up was a masterstroke. He finally undertook a vast, 16-month world tour, which broke box office records around the globe.

His total of 123 sell-out concerts thrilled four and a half million people, and earned $125 million. In the UK, his seven full-capacity shows at Wembley Stadium were also unprecedented in their scale. John Peel's review for the *Observer* described them as "stupendous... resembling some futuristic technological pantomime." Jackson was growing into being the greatest living showman. Yet, the always candid Quincy Jones found Michael's ability to switch

Below Michael was still – mostly – on good terms with his brothers.

Opposite Meet the press – Michael's record-breaking tours met a feverish response.

Following page Of Jackson's Wembley Stadium shows, John Peel wrote, "Stupendous…a futuristic technological pantomime".

“He can go out and perform in front of 90,000 people, but if I ask him to sing a song for me, I have to sit on the couch with my hands over my eyes [...] He is amazingly shy.

on the charisma and the moves in front of gigantic crowds amusing. "He can go out and perform in front of 90,000 people," he mused, "but if I ask him to sing a song for me, I have to sit on the couch with my hands over my eyes, and then he goes behind the couch. He is amazingly shy."

Nevertheless, Michael kept fanning the flames of his fame. The hits (and expensive videos) kept coming – 'Bad', 'The Way You Make Me Feel', 'I Just Can't Stop Loving You', 'Dirty Diana', 'Smooth Criminal', 'Man In The Mirror' (all the profits from which were donated to charity) and 'Liberian Girl'. There were some who rated *Bad* as an even greater album than *Thriller*, with *Rolling Stone* deeming it "richer and sexier", calling Michael "a gifted singer-songwriter with his own skewed aesthetic". So dominant was he that when his sister, Janet, properly launched her music career with the excellent *Control* album, it's rumoured he complained: "I want to be the only Jackson on the charts." His competitive instincts had also led him to try to get rising superstar Prince to collaborate, but Prince gracefully declined an offer to duet on 'Bad'. Barbra Streisand, too, decided that duetting on 'I Just Can't Stop Loving You' might be "unconvincing". He'd fallen out with Diana Ross after a row, so his management sounded out Aretha Franklin and Whitney Houston. In the end, the then-unknown Siedah Garrett, a Quincy find who'd co-authored 'Man In The Mirror' landed the role, and shone in it. So much so that gossiping papers presumed a romance between Michael and Siedah, two years his junior. "Jackson And Lookalike Mull Marriage!" shrieked one headline, implausibly. They were just friends, and Garrett sang on subsequent tours. The rapport lasted until she sang on Madonna records and shows, at which point a disgruntled Michael considered her to have defected to a "rival".

Michael's new image hadn't wowed everybody, however. Some sneered at his (much) whiter skin, and how radically altered the shape of his face had been since the innocent visage of the *Off The Wall* days. And the near-constant crotch-grabbing and yelping became a point of mockery for sceptics. Even Quincy quipped, "Is his underwear too tight?" You can see why this was the last album Jackson and Jones collaborated on. At the same time, it got people talking – the hype was heated. Another fictional romance was invented by reporters linking Michael to his co-star and object of lusty affections in the 'The Way You Make Me Feel' video, Tatiana Thumbtzen. She'd seen off thousands of other girls' auditions to take the part, sashaying her way elegantly to four days of shooting at a thousand dollars a day. There was some merit in the conjecture, as she was invited onto the *Bad* tour and admitted to a crush on her "boss" – but it was apparently unrequited. A shared kiss onstage at Madison Square Garden excited the press – they labelled her "Michael's Girl" – but didn't sit well with management head Frank DiLeo, who was aware that fans had never seen their idol kissed by a girl before. Tatiana claimed she was dropped from the tour for this, but was at least given a consoling hug by Michael's mother. Her replacement was a young, up-and-coming Sheryl Crow. Needless

Above The donning of surgical masks was just one of the traits which caused the "Wacko Jacko" tag.

Right Shy in person, charismatic on stage, reckoned Quincy Jones.

to say, the media got to work on false rumours that Sheryl was now dating Michael. Tatiana, for her part, went on to date Prince.

Into his crammed diary, Michael shoehorned an acting role in esteemed director Francis Ford Coppola's sci-fi musical short, *Captain Eo*, playing the title character. Produced in 3D by George Lucas, this was a high-budget venture and Michael and all involved must have envisaged it making a big impact. It didn't, although Disney ran it in Florida for many years. While it never made much impact on the history of cinema, it was on a promo obligation for *Captain Eo* that Michael first wore a surgical mask over his face in public. The reports of his eccentricity went ding-a-ling. He'd been reading about the notorious recluse Howard Hughes and, yes, there was initially a degree of pop-star affectation about his sartorial choice. Get 'em talking, and all that. But to an extent, the "Michael Jackson Is Weird" label became a runaway train, and exploded out of its

Left Rumours of romance between the King and Queen (Madonna) of Pop were greatly exaggerated.

Right *Moonwalker* the movie only made a slight profit.

Below Tea for two: Bubbles the chimp shares a cuppa.

central character's control. For example, the *New Musical Express* review of *Bad* by John McCready suggested that many had little interest in the music, writing about the myths that abounded: "He bathes in Perrier and wants to build his own Buckingham Palace. He asked David Hockney to paint Diana Ross's face on the bottom of his swimming pool. He hopes to live until he's 150... such stories, created by an unholy alliance of Encino aides with a strange sense of loyalty... help convince a pop audience, for whom music is never enough, that Michael Jackson and the real world of alarm clocks and dirty socks do not belong together." Such was the publicity team's pyrotechnic display that 'Dirty Diana' was said by some to be a dig at Diana Ross, and by others, even more oddly, to be about Princess Diana.

After a flop or two in the film world, Michael finally got his bearings in that arena with 1988's *Moonwalker*. This decidedly off-the-wall mix of concert footage, videos, biographical snippets, animation sequences and surreal fantasy topped the *Billboard* video chart for over five months. Moreover, the video which eventually took its number-one spot was *Michael Jackson: The Legend Continues*. Jackson had dreamt of releasing *Moonwalker* to cinemas globally, but was advised that financially a direct-to-video release was the sounder idea. He was therefore displeased, despite its strong chart showing, when its $27 million dollars budget brought just $30 million in sales. Along with the fact that *Bad* hadn't outsold *Thriller* – bear in mind, however, that it had become the second biggest selling album in history – this led to him demanding that John Branca fire manager Frank DiLeo. DiLeo later described Jackson as "part Howard Hughes, part E.T."

The film was directed by Chris Chilvers, who called Michael "a perfectionist. I knew it would be difficult, and it was." It featured Joe "Goodfellas" Pesci, a then 12-year-old Sean Lennon – John's son and for a time, good friends with Jackson – and brief shots of Elizabeth Taylor and Mick Jagger. The key sequences of its 93 minutes were the renditions of 'Smooth Criminal' and 'Leave Me Alone', each also released as individual videos. 'Speed Demon' and a version of The Beatles' 'Come Together' (well, he did own the rights) also stood out. Michael had hoped to superimpose himself over a vintage Fred Astaire movie scene, dancing opposite Fred in place of Ginger Rogers, but Astaire's widow denied him permission.

There was also the book *Moonwalk*, a none too candid set of memoirs and musings from Michael. He'd been persuaded to do it by another celebrity pal, Jackie Onassis, the former First Lady Jackie Kennedy, who was an editor at the New York publishing house, Doubleday. Even Michael – not one for confessionals – couldn't resist Jackie's charm, and her cunning pitch

Opposite It's a kind of magic: Michael levitates.

Below Michael is taken into hospital with severe burns to the head after the shooting of a commercial in Los Angeles.

Following pages Waxing lyrical – Michael visits Madame Tussaud's in London, 1985.

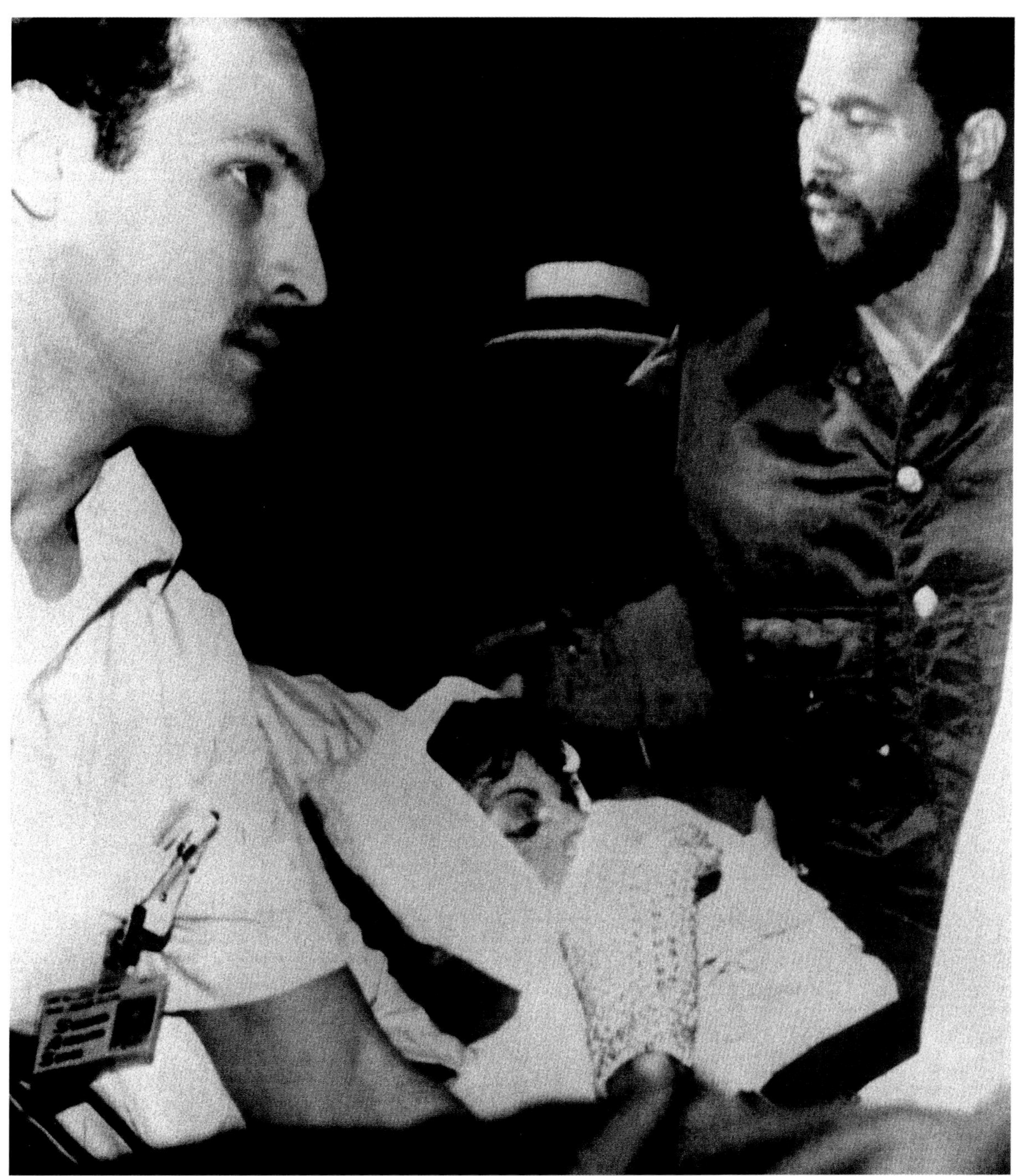

MADAME

Hollywood
FAME

was: "Just be Peter Pan. That's all you have to do." That said, he stood her up at their first intended meeting about the book, and she was furious. You didn't stand Jackie O up, no matter who you were. They overcame this inauspicious start, with Michael admitting, "Jackie twisted my arm." The project was realized and topped the *New York Times* best-seller list, shifting over half a million copies. Jackie wrote, with some spin given that she was promoting the tome, "To many people Michael Jackson seems an elusive personality, but to those who work with him he is not. This talented artist is a sensitive man, warm, funny and full of insight. *Moonwalk* provides a startling glimpse of the artist at work and in reflection." The ghost writers did their best, finding a few nuggets regarding Michael's lonely youth. He felt awkward about the criticisms of his father therein, and in fact phoned Joseph to apologize. He also finally came clean about having had two rhinoplastic surgeries and that new cleft chin, which, it transpired, was inspired by watching old Kirk Douglas films. He dedicated the book to Fred Astaire.

Michael's amended appearance and image were still drawing criticism, as a *Rolling Stone* readers' poll voted him "worst hype" and "worst dressed". Sensitive as ever, he took flak like this to heart, not built for a backlash, too thin-skinned to brush it off. Awards were still coming in by the truckload, more happily, from the Brits to the American Music Awards, though he wasn't over the moon when Janet pipped him to one award with her 'When I Think Of You' video. The Grammys were a major blow to his ego. Despite performing 'The Way You Make Me Feel' and 'Man In The Mirror' at the ceremony, his first televised appearance for five years, he won nothing. When Diana Ross, of all people, awarded the Best Album trophy to U2 for *The Joshua Tree*, it was said that he collapsed backstage and threw out accusations of racism.

He'd often retreat, when not travelling on tour, to Neverland, the expansive 2,700-acre ranch he'd

Opposite A star on Hollywood's walk of fame was inevitable.

Above Jackson with President Ronald Reagan and First Lady Nancy.

Following pages: Left above: The Reverend Jesse Jackson greets Michael, his brother Marlon (left) and father Joe (right). **Left below:** With enduring close friend and screen legend Elizabeth Taylor at the American Music Awards, 1986. **Right:** The Jackson–Jones creative partnership produced some of the era's finest music.

bought in Santa Barbara, California, for a rumoured $30 million, and moved in full-time in November 1988. He left the family abode in Hayvenhurst – described by Jackie O as "like La La Land, with animals in cages and a damn chimpanzee running amok" – for somewhere that made "La La Land" seem eminently conventional by comparison. Michael soon had it kitted out with a zoo hosting pythons and tarantulas, railroads and trains, an amusement park which included a Ferris wheel, a carousel, a rollercoaster, dodgems and a cinema, and employed fifty staff. Ideally, he'd have liked to enact all his frustrated childhood dreams here, as the name, taken from *Peter Pan*, suggested. It was a place where he did not have to grow up.

Eight miles from the nearest town or, as Michael put it, "a thirty-minute helicopter ride from Los Angeles", it had previously been owned by a golf course entrepreneur. Michael had first fallen in love with it on a visit there with Paul and Linda McCartney some years previously. He invited stars like Steven Seagal and Bo Derek to his housewarming party, but not his parents. Macaulay Culkin, with whom Michael bonded over child stardom, was a frequent guest. "It was a child's dream," he said poignantly. "We're both going to be eight years old forever in some place, because we never had a chance to be eight when we actually were."

Neverland wasn't cheap to maintain. Michael's earnings were vast, but so was his expenditure. Sure, his wealth was once valued at a billion, and over the eighties his royalties came to over $250 million. The addition of some Elvis Presley songs to his Beatles catalogue gave him a huge annual publishing income. But he was not one to baulk at high prices, and spent flamboyantly. The touring was bringing in more money, and people around the world were flocking to see the superstar's dazzling show. Yet it cost more than it made, what with Michael's taste for private planes and desire to ramp up the show's razzle-dazzle whatever the price.

Those attending would see state-of-the-art lasers, magic illusions inspired by Michael's admiration for his friends Uri Geller and David Blaine, and a

Left On any stage, Michael was completely in his element.

Previous pages: Left When you win that many awards, it's best to have your glove on. **Right** Michael at the 1984 Grammy Awards, with actress Brooke Shields and young actor Emmanuel Lewis. Jackson and Shields were the subject of much media speculation, and were rumoured to be in a relationship at the time.

> “I collapsed; I fainted. I cancelled my show because I simply could not perform. I broke down and wept for weeks afterwards.

spectacular sequence where it almost appeared he was flying as he hung suspended on high from a crane. The real magic, however, remained his own showmanship. Prince Charles and Princess Diana were among those who attended his Wembley Stadium shows and when they met, Michael joked to Prince Charles that he could give him dance lessons. Princess Diana had danced vigorously to 'Dirty Diana', and Michael sang her praises. They developed a telephone friendship, discussing ways to avoid the paparazzi. "In my heart," gushed Michael, "I was saying: I love you, Diana! Shine! You are the true princess of the people!" Upon her sad death in 1997, he sighed, "I collapsed; I fainted. I cancelled my show because I simply could not perform. I broke down and wept for weeks afterwards. She used to confide in me – she felt hunted and trapped just the way I do."

He felt a kinship with the very, very famous, and indeed with royalty. Around this time – irritated that Elvis had bagged the nickname The King – he took on the moniker The King of Pop, a name suggested, it's been claimed, by his regal friend and screen icon Elizabeth Taylor. "He is not really of this planet," she said affectionately. "He is larger than life... a genius, a living legend, a megastar. There's no one can come near him. No one can dance like that, or write lyrics like that, or cause the kind of excitement that he does."

When the *Bad* tour finished in January 1989, he'd excited fifteen countries, across four continents. Japan called him "Typhoon Michael". Australia was more keen on the "Wacko Jacko" angle, while USA's *Today* plumped for "Raw sex". Michael penned a defensive letter to *People* magazine, which requested: "Do not judge a man until you've walked two moons in his moccasins." He befriended Dreamworks mogul

---

Above Michael's stadium gigs, such as this one at Páirc Uí Chaoimh in Cork, Ireland, were massive logistical operations.

Left Michael sports a military-inspired get-up at yet another awards show in 1986.

David Geffen, but never found the perfect-fit movie role he sought. Rumours of his casting in a Spielberg production of *The Phantom of the Opera* led to naught. And as the eighties drew to a close, Jackson even fired his attorney John Branca, the canny businessman to whom many attribute his widespread commercial success. (Unknown to the singer, Branca was at that moment on the brink of acquiring him the rights to James Brown's back catalogue, a long-held ambition). Taking advice from Geffen, Jackson installed Sandy Gallin as his new manager. These dramatic moves fuelled chatter that Michael was planning to buy Motown from Berry Gordy, but it was reported that they couldn't agree on the price.

Newspapers also drummed up that "romance" with his tour singer Sheryl Crow, but she laughed. "He never took that glove off for me." Next came the media's dream date, as Michael and Madonna had a "rendezvous" at an L.A. restaurant, The Ivy. Both wore photogenic outfits, and it gave off the vibrations of a stellar arranged summit meeting between The King and Queen of Pop, more than anything of amorous potential. They left in separate limos, but they did attend the 63rd Oscars ceremony together, with wags noting that Michael wore two gloves, as if to shield himself from Madge's advances. Andrew Morton's *Madonna* biography purports that she attempted a seduction shortly after the Oscars, but "he was giggling too much. This was one man she was not able to conquer."

Michael had, however, conquered the eighties, and then some. As he watched his brothers' careers struggle to soar without him, he accepted the Artist of the Decade award from Elizabeth Taylor, and was named Most Important Entertainer of the Year 1989 by *Entertainment Tonight*. *Rolling Stone*, atoning somewhat for its bouts of mickey-taking, cited *Thriller* as Album of the Decade and, not to be outdone, President George H. W. Bush invited Jackson to the White House to be honoured as Entertainer of the Decade. Could he possibly sustain this level of fame and acclaim into the nineties? "They ain't seen nothin' yet," he told David Geffen. "I'll double my success."

Below It's gospel: Michael performs with a host of backing singers.

Opposite Promoting Pepsi with hair safely out of reach of errant flames.

PEPSI

THE 1990s

Michael's next album, 1991's *Dangerous*, was another commercial blockbuster, and his tour of the same name again broke records. Yet this was to be a tempestuous decade for The King of Pop, as perceptions of his curious personality and two marriages led to increasingly feverish press coverage, often a mixture of half-truths and fiction which disturbed the star almost as much as his unpredictable life choices disturbed the media.

It started swimmingly, with Jackson signing a new contract with Sony, which varying reports described as the best deal for any artist in recording history. A "fifteen-year six-album deal" was cited, with some heated journalists claiming it was worth a billion dollars to the singer. That was inaccurate, but as the biggest star in the world Jackson did receive a previously unparalleled royalty rate: it's been calculated that over the next fifteen years, he took home $175 million from album sales through this agreement.

Perhaps a touch of jealousy, therefore, crept into Jermaine Jackson's psyche when, in 1991, he took a snipe at his younger brother. "I could have been Michael," he moaned. "It's all a matter of timing and luck." Pushing things further, he released the less-than-gracious single 'Word To The Badd', in which he asked, "Once you were made, you changed your shade/ Was your colour wrong?" Michael was understandably incensed, and in a phone call to his mother suggested she banish Jermaine from Hayvenhurst, where the family still lived, and a property which Michael mostly owned still. Katharine kept the peace, but from then on – for a while – Jermaine was asked to leave the house whenever Michael made a rare visit. The brothers did bury the hatchet in later years. Jermaine spun the message of the song as "an older brother telling a younger brother to get back to reality".

In fact, Jermaine's song was completely overshadowed by Michael's own new single, released the same week, which dealt with skin colour in a relatively more subtle way. 'Black Or White', a global smash with an "event" video and cutting rock-guitar riff from Guns N' Roses' Slash, seemed to both advocate racial equality and implicitly argue that Michael's own shadings mattered less than his musical actions. It was his biggest hit since 'Billie Jean'. *Dangerous* was a different beast to the three previous album phenomena, in that it saw Quincy Jones replaced as producer by the young R&B/ swingbeat tyros Teddy Riley and Bill Bottrell (Jackson

Below Suited and booted, but still crotch-grabbing. MTV Video Awards 1995.

Right From riches to rags: well, he had played The Scarecrow in *The Wiz*.

co-produced). Recorded in LA across over a year of sessions, it was, at 77 minutes, effectively a double album. It marked an evolution in sound for Michael, updating his grooves and arrangements for a younger audience, and spawned hit singles such as 'In The Closet', 'Remember The Time', 'Jam' and the epic eco-ballad 'Heal The World'. Despite a retina-scorching psychedelic sleeve and just one Grammy award (a disappointment for Jackson), as well as 300,000 copies being stolen by an armed gang at LA Airport a few days before release, it sold over 32 million copies. When the Grammys gave him a "Grammy Legend" Award in 1993, it seemed as if they were compensating for not giving it sufficient acclaim. His sister, Janet, now a superstar herself, presented this award, and Michael joked, "See? Me and Janet really are two different people!"

The Dangerous world tour was marketed as "the most spectacular, state-of-the-art show the world has ever seen". It was again sponsored by Pepsi, who paid Michael in the region of $20 million, and was planned to run from June 1992 to November 1993, this time visiting even Africa – Michael's first visit there since teenage days. However, Michael suffered a problem with his vocal cords, and delays and cancellations ensued. This can be costly when your touring entourage and staff number 235 people. A Bucharest show was filmed and screened on HBO, and Jackson donated profits to his Heal the World foundation and other charities. Halfway through the tour, on 31 January 1993, Michael performed at the Pasadena Rose Bowl for the prestigious NFL Super Bowl half-time show, attracting what was, at the time, the highest-ever TV audience for the event estimated at a dizzying 133 million.

There was still a backlash: one reviewer, for example said Jackson was "unable to face the fresh challenges of the nineties... he reiterates the clichés that served him well in the eighties." The record's experimental elements didn't go down well with everybody, and perhaps aggrieved by this, Michael didn't release an all-new studio album for another decade. Ever striving to outdo his own greatness, he'd put plenty into *Dangerous*. "I wanted to do an album that was like Tchaikovsky's *Nutcracker Suite*," he declared straight-

Opposite Madonna, still trying to justify her love, attends the 1991 Oscars with Michael.

Above The man in the mask: Michael beats it.

BETACAM
3CCD
SONY
FUJINON

faced. "So that a thousand years from now people would still be listening to it. Something that would live forever. I would like to see children and teenagers and parents and races all over the world, hundreds and hundreds of years from now, still pulling out songs from that album and dissecting it. I want it to live on."

His own life was growing ever more turbulent. (In the 1995 single 'Scream', which co-starred Janet, he hollered, almost as a cry for help, "Stop pressuring me!") The media stories about his Wacko Jacko persona had spread too thick and fast for him or his managers to control. People became immune to shock; it was as if the public shrugged and decided that when it came to Michael, they'd just believe anything, however unlikely and far-fetched. Scandal, gossip, rumour and blatant fantasy piled up on front pages everywhere. "Why not just tell people I'm an alien from Mars?"

Opposite Leave Me Alone? The media were never likely to obey Michael's request.

Left The face had taken on an angular quality.

Below With Donald Trump, later to become President of the USA.

Following pages Black Or White – Michael leaps into action.

> “I have a skin disorder that destroys the pigmentation. It’s something I can’t help, OK? When people make up stories that I don’t want to be what I am, it hurts me.

he protested to one journalist. "Tell them I eat live chickens and do a voodoo dance at midnight. They'll believe anything you say, because you're a reporter." Michael vented further, and with some logic. "But if I, Michael Jackson, were to say, 'I'm an alien from Mars and I eat live chickens and do a voodoo dance at midnight' people would say, 'Oh, man, that Michael Jackson is nuts! He's cracked up! You can't believe a damn word that comes out of his mouth!' "

Of course it was chiefly the mutations in his appearance which fuelled the fire. He argued that, "All of Hollywood has plastic surgery! I don't know why the press picks me out. It's just my nose, you know..." On another occasion he reflected sadly, "Wacko Jacko – where did that come from? I have a heart and I have feelings. I feel that, when you do that to me. It's not nice. Don't do it. I'm not a 'wacko'." In a February 1993 TV interview with a sympathetic Oprah Winfrey, where he was more frank and open than usual, he targeted those who said he was "bleaching" his skin in order to appear more "white". "I have a skin disorder that destroys the pigmentation," he offered candidly. "It's something I can't help, OK? When people make up stories that I don't want to be what I am, it hurts me." In the same interview, he spoke again of loneliness during his childhood. He also declared that he was still dating Brooke Shields, and in support of this semi-truth, she did go to the Grammys with him that year. Michael had enjoyed another trip to the White House as well, invited to President Bill Clinton's inauguration ball in January 1993 by the new president and his family. He and other stars sang a celebratory 'We Are The World', and Clinton's daughter, Chelsea, was "ecstatic" about meeting her pop idol.

Brooke Shields, however, was apparently still just a friend doing another friend a favour, as opposed to a lover. In terms of Michael Jackson's love life, the big

Below Legends of soul – Stevie Wonder, Aretha Franklin, Michael, Diana Ross.

Opposite A dramatic pose is always enhanced by a wind machine.

Following Pages Michael's intensity on stage never wavered, despite a physically and emotionally demanding tour schedule.

“Why not just tell people I’m an alien from Mars? Tell them I eat live chickens? They’ll believe anything you say if you’re a reporter…

story broke in 1994. It surprised everybody when, out of the blue, The King of Pop married the daughter of The King, Elvis Presley.

It came at a peculiar time, as Michael faced crises and court cases, with early rumours of his painkiller addiction swirling and Pepsi withdrawing $35 million worth of sponsorship from a cancelled tour. As turmoil raged like a tornado, Michael grew closer to someone he'd first met in 1975 at a Jacksons concert in Las Vegas. On 26 May 1994, he married Lisa-Marie Presley in a private wedding in the Dominican Republic. The privacy didn't last – as the couple must have foreseen, their union was the media's wildest fantasy. The heiress to The King of Rock 'n' Roll (whose catalogue Jackson retained an interest in) marrying the enigmatic King of Pop? The headlines needed no kick-start. Many detected a large hint of a publicity stunt, designed to distract them from Jackson's troubles and reboot his much-questioned sexual identity. It was, they suggested, a set-up to make him seem more "normal", a regular married Joe. There was of course a frenzy of speculation. For his part, Michael cooed, "I'm really learning the real meaning of love." He spoke of how it would last, but he and Lisa-Marie were divorced by January 1996.

As startling as the marriage was, it also made a kind of sense on some levels. Lisa-Marie understood fame as well as anybody, having witnessed its effects close-hand more than most, and would have been able to relate to Michael's pressurized situation. Born in Memphis, in 1968, the only child of Elvis and Priscilla Presley, she lived at Graceland until her parents' divorce when she was five. She then moved between Graceland (perhaps an inspiration for Neverland) and her mother's place in Beverly Hills. She knew vast riches, and Elvis' private jet bore her name. After Elvis's death in 1977, she had a stormy relationship with Priscilla, who she claimed was too often away shooting her role in TV show *Dallas*. She accused her mother's new partner of inappropriate advances. By 20, she was married for the first time, to musician and ongoing confidante Danny Keogh, with whom she had two children, Danielle Riley and Bridget Storm. She and Keogh divorced in 1994, remaining good friends, and just twenty days later she married Jackson. "Things moved very quickly," she said. No kidding.

They'd been talking frequently on the phone, bonding, and Liz Taylor revealed that Michael had told her in earlier times that he'd fallen in love with Lisa-

Left While his private life was suffering, Michael continued to deliver on stage.

Marie and wanted to marry her. He proposed during one lengthy phone call. Lisa-Marie proudly stated that he "needed" her. "Someone young and vibrant, like me. My future is ahead of me. And his is ahead of him." When they were both in Vegas, in February 1994 – Michael filming *The Jackson Family Honors* TV special at the MGM Grand – he took her to a Temptations show, holding her hand. One Donald Trump (whatever happened to him?) said, "They looked like any other lovey-dovey couple to me." Lisa spent time at Neverland, with her children, and Michael was pleased to see she got on well with animals. "Friends" were quoted as saying she was crazy for him, and that he was showering her with flowers and gifts.

Those who dismissed the romance as a cynical publicity campaign had the wind taken out of their sails when the news of the marriage wasn't revealed until after the small ceremony and a honeymoon at the Casa De Campo resort. Michael and Lisa-Marie had genuinely enjoyed some private time. Liz Taylor threw journalists off the scent by scoffing, "That's the most ridiculous thing I've ever heard! Michael is a sane and reasonable man. He's not crazy!" The apparently crazy-in-love newly-weds visited Disney World together, and Lisa-Marie said they'd kept it secret to prevent a "happy occasion" becoming a "media circus". Now the headlines broke – "the odd couple marriage of the century!" – but Lisa-Marie kept her sassy cool: "Elvis liked to wear uniforms. So does Michael. Elvis loved amusement parks. Michael has his own amusement park."

It was certainly a rollercoaster romance, even if it wasn't all fun and games. Michael contradicted the initial story by claiming he'd proposed to Lisa-Marie in his lounge at Neverland after they'd watched a screening together of their favourite film, the classic Bette Davis movie *All About Eve*. With regard to the scandals hounding Michael, and the reports of his excessive prescription drugs intake (initially brought on by his Pepsi ad burnt-hair accident, he claimed), Lisa-Marie protested, "I believed he didn't do anything wrong. And that he was wrongly accused. So I started falling for him. I wanted to save him... I felt I could."

Left Smooth, or criminal? Michael's outfits divided fashion pundits.

Opposite Speak no evil – the guarded superstar maintains mystery.

Following pages: Left above On the Dangerous tour of 1992 and 1993, one of Michael's costumes was that of a gold-clad astronaut. **Left below** The man, in the mirror. **Right** Space Age guitar hero.

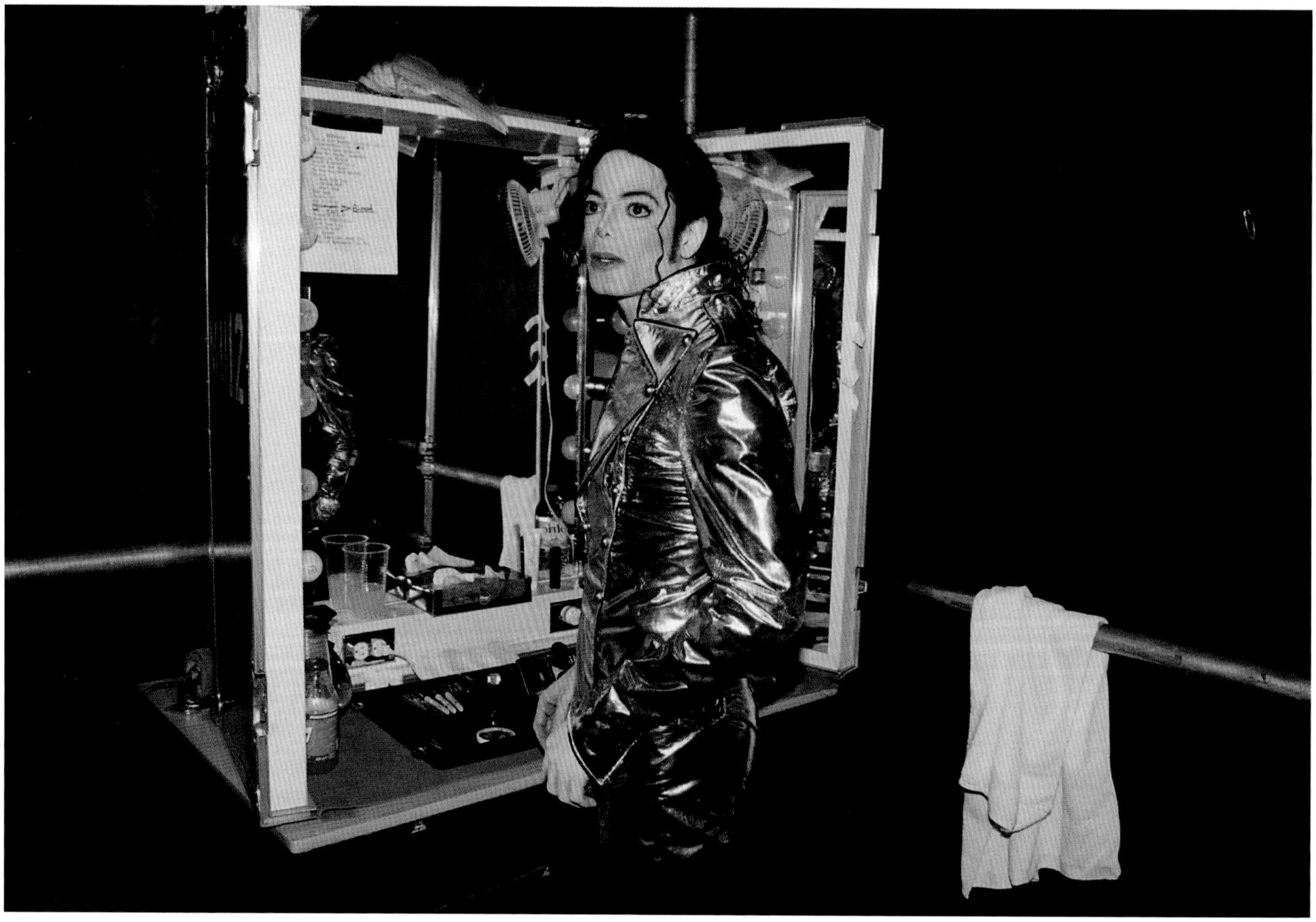

She encouraged him to settle the Chandler case – which we'll come to shortly – out of court, and to seek help for his medication issues. (When Michael died in 2009, she released a statement expressing a sense that she'd failed to save him from the "inevitable".)

The couple had delivered a very public display of steamy affection in the video for Michael's single 'You Are Not Alone', smooching scantily-dressed. They attended the MTV Video Music Awards at Radio City Music Hall in New York, and again kissed heartily in view of a massive TV audience. And, in June 1995, to tie in with the release of Michael's next album *HIStory*, they appeared on Diane Sawyer's ABC show together. They reiterated that they'd first met when very young then bonded later, and stated a dream of having children together: surely a rock-pop genetic masterstroke. Lisa-Marie got quite animated when dismissing the "showmance" gossip. "Why would I marry someone I didn't love?" she appealed. "I admire and respect him, and love him." The highlight of the interview had to be when the feisty Lisa-Marie demanded of the host: "Do we have sex? Go ahead! Is that what you wanted to ask? Yes, yes, yes!" A bold announcement: however, Michael disturbed the erotic idyll by barking of the Chandler allegations, "That whole thing is a lie!" His outburst broke a confidentiality agreement, and only motivated the Chandlers onto opening further proceedings.

Lisa-Marie's passion seemingly cooled thereafter, as she took a vacation in Hawaii with her ex-husband Danny Keogh and her children; and when Michael was admitted to hospital after taking ill while shooting the HBO TV special *One Night Only*, her visit there included a discussion about divorce. She was well recompensed financially, and agreed never to "kiss and tell" in print. The divorce officially occurred on 18 January 1996. "Irreconcilable differences" were cited. In 2005, she was supportive at a Jackson trial and, in 2010, she told Oprah Winfrey that they'd remained friends for the next few years, and that she'd still sometimes travelled across the world to be with him. (She went on to marry screen star Nicolas Cage, a marriage that lasted 108 days, then musician Michael Lockwood, now her fourth divorce.)

Opposite Environmental compassion: Michael in the "Heal The World" video.

Above A white-clad Michael on stage with a chorus of children at the 1996 Brit Awards in London.

The unsavoury legal issues that had clouded Michael and Lisa-Marie's time together had begun with the Chandler family accusing the singer of abusing their 13-year-old son, Jordan. Jackson denied this vehemently: "I'd slit my wrists before I hurt a child… I could never do that. No one will ever know how much these wicked rumours have hurt me." The press had a field day, though the case never went to trial, with Jackson settling out of court, paying out a multi-million dollar sum. Lisa-Marie had encouraged this, but if the intent was to make the scandal go away, it arguably only increased suspicion. The friendship between Jackson and Chandler had involved visits to Neverland, and even an outing to a Monaco awards ceremony, where the pair dressed identically. When police and prosecutors opened their investigations, headlines shrieked, "Is He Dangerous Or Just Off The Wall?". The decade had taken an unpleasant turn. Michael was deeply upset, cancelling concerts, increasing his painkiller doses, sending Liz Taylor a cry for help. She predicted "vindication", mentioning the word "extortion". Michael's 35th birthday was miserable, as he emotionally vowed never to return to Los Angeles. Fans rallied round loyally, and celebrities did too, at least at first. But when the police raided Hayvenhurst, Michael was so depressed that it took all his willpower and professionalism to get through pre-arranged concerts. That leg of the tour finished, he flew to the UK by private jet, hoping Britain might prove a temporary sanctuary. He released a statement referring again to "extortion" and "false allegations", saying he was left "physically and emotionally exhausted", admitting to his painkiller dependency, and cancelling future live dates. "I know I can overcome the problem and will be stronger from the experience", he concluded. Sony declared "unconditional and unwavering support".

Michael did return to LA, but Neverland was under siege from paparazzi and reporters. His nightmare plumbed new depths when he was strip-searched and photographed by police, but he was determined to prove his innocence. "Don't treat me like a criminal, because I am innocent." When the settlement was agreed, Michael's image was wounded, though not as harshly as his morale. "The time has come for Michael to get on with his life," announced his lawyer. And after licking his scars, he did that, pushing forward with the album *HIStory*, a mix of greatest hits and new material. The new single 'Scream' indicated his stress and paranoia, the memorable monochrome video with his sister a shriek of protest. The album sold twenty million, possibly not as many copies as hoped, but a respectable figure given the recent controversies, and its inclusion of repackaged old songs. Michael's next move definitely shifted focus, as the revelation came that he had a new wife and partner, the previously unknown Debbie Rowe.

"Debbie Who?" spluttered the newspapers. "Who the hell is she?" barked Madonna. Even hardcore fans never saw this one coming. A Washington-born nurse, just four months younger than Michael, she'd first met the star at Dr. Arnold Klein's dermatology clinic in the eighties, when he'd had treatment for vitiligo. She'd helped him medically with the condition ever since. She recalled that after Michael's divorce from Lisa-Marie, he'd been saddened that he might never be a father. Lisa-Marie was later to say she always felt Debbie had a crush on Michael. In 1996, Debbie became pregnant, and she and Michael married on 14 November. (She'd been previously married, for six years, from 1982–88). On 13 February

Above Michael and Lisa Marie Presley together in happier times.

Right The Dangerous tour had helped the album of the same name become the biggest seller of 1992.

“ Michael Jackson is still big. If the genre got small, that’s hardly his fault.

1997, Michael Joseph Jackson Jr was born in Los Angeles, his nickname of Prince later sticking. (The rivalry between Jackson and the artist Prince appeared to have mellowed into respect: it’s said that Prince even had a nickname for Michael: “Camille”). On 3 April 1998, a daughter, Paris Jackson, was born.

Yet, by October 1999, Debbie and Michael were divorced. Rowe, previously not remotely a celebrity, had felt overwhelmed and stressed by the avalanche of publicity and scrutiny that came with being Michael’s wife. She signed full custody of the two children to Jackson, though, in 2005 she was allowed limited visiting rights after the star’s further in-court troubles.

At first she was stoic. “I’d never do this for money,” she retorted to the inevitable cynics. “I did this because I love him. And that’s the only reason.” Katharine Jackson had apparently encouraged the couple to marry, and the venue – Michael’s suite at the Sheraton In The Park in Sydney, Australia – was chosen for privacy reasons. Debbie’s ring was a two-and-a-half carat diamond, set into platinum. “I’m on top of the world,” she declared. She perhaps tempted fate when saying, “My friendship with him is the most important thing to me, and if this marriage gets in the way of that, then we’ll put the marriage aside.” Michael was equally (possibly unwisely) frank, when he gushed that he was so excited when Paris was born that he tried to leave the hospital with her instantly, wrapping her in a blanket, placenta and all. As the children grew up, they were granted rather more discretion, often to the point of being hidden from public view or masked or veiled when in it.

Meanwhile, Michael continued to rehabilitate his career. The launch of *HIStory* had involved giant forty-foot-tall statue-like effigies of Jackson, floated along major rivers in big European cities, the one sailing on the Thames in London drawing a big splash of attention. He picked up his punishing touring schedule, and when he played a packed Wembley Stadium in July 1997, this writer reviewed it breathlessly, using words like "stellar", "radiant", "both acrobat and preacher" and "giddy rapture". "Michael Jackson is still big," I pontificated. "If the genre got small, that's hardly his fault."

That year also saw another album, though again it was a mix of old and new. *Blood On The Dance Floor* (subtitled *HIStory In The Mix*) featured eight remixes of tracks from HIStory, plus five new songs. The fresh title song, a single that gave him his last UK number one of his lifetime, was as lithe and nimble as some of his best work, rediscovering his groove's crackle and sass, though tracks like 'Morphine' and 'Ghosts' alluded to the darker side of being Michael Jackson. The album went platinum. At this stage, Michael was still earning tens of millions per year. Separately, in 1999 his parents filed for bankruptcy, but Michael himself had appointed a new manager, a member of the Saudi royal family, no less: Prince Alwaleed. He and Jackson developed Kingdom Entertainment, involving interests in hotels, restaurants, theme parks and film projects. The "Michael Jackson And Friends" charity concerts in Germany and Korea raised vast sums, and he performed for War Child, in aid of Kosovan refugees, with Luciano Pavarotti, in Italy. Michael also raised big money for UNESCO, the Red Cross and Nelson Mandela's Children's Fund: he met Mandela in South Africa, and the iconic pair posed happily for photographs together. The nineties, then, had been difficult for Michael compared to the euphoric eighties, but he appeared to be bouncing back with resilience and a rediscovered sense of fun, perhaps boosted by fatherhood. He looked forward to a new century with some optimism.

Opposite Top-hatted Guns N' Roses guitarist Slash gets down onstage with a rocking Michael.

Below Michael had dreamed of staying young forever in Neverland.

Following pages Russia with love – Michael was rarely one to skimp on promotional budgets.

THE 2000s

The twenty-first century began with renewed momentum for Jackson, with his 2001 album *Invincible* – a comeback album in the sense that it was his first all-new material collection since *Dangerous* a decade previous – swiftly reaching double platinum status. A success by anyone else's standards, but no *Thriller*. Of course the media portrayed this high-budget release as a flop, and the ever-sensitive Jackson took it to heart. He butted heads with Sony boss Tommy Mottola over the marketing campaign, calling him a "devil" who should "go back to hell", and even going so far as to accuse him of bordering on racism by not promoting it as much as a white artist's record. This ill-advised attack only drew a defensive retort from Sony, who stated they'd spent a fortune on a "disappointing" album. In this case, even the distinguished civil-rights activist the Rev. Al Sharpton took Mottola's side. "Music moguls are liars," seethed Jackson. "They manipulate history. If you go to the record store on the corner, you won't see one black face. You'll see Elvis Presley and the Rolling Stones. The attack on me began after I broke Elvis' and The Beatles' sales." He continued, revealing perhaps the real cause of his wrath. "It's a conspiracy. I was called a freak, a homosexual and a child molester." Little wonder, given this toxic acrimony, that the deal between Sony and the singer ended soon afterwards.

"I'd rather receive praise from my fans than think about the people on my enemy list," grumbled Jackson, who, in March 2001, enjoyed respite from the feuding by accepting induction into the Rock and Roll Hall of Fame in New York, the youngest person ever to receive that honour. Also that month, he surprised many by showing up at Oxford University in the UK to launch the Heal the Kids charity. Speaking at the university's Student Union, he burst into tears in front of stunned onlookers. "I wanted to be a typical little boy," he confided, oversharing, reflecting on his roots. "But my father had it otherwise. All I could do was envy the laughter and playtime that seemed to be going on all around me... All of us are a product of our childhoods, but I am the product of a lack of childhood. If you don't have the memory of being loved, you are condemned to search the world for something to fill you up." While such outbursts of vulnerability didn't dilute the Wacko Jacko accusations, they did remind everyone of his difficult, unconventional upbringing.

Invincible was, for all the flak, churning out hit singles, and Michael capitalized by organizing two sell-out televised shows in September at Madison Square Garden, New York, to celebrate his thirty years in show business. The subsequent TV screenings drew over forty million viewers, a record for the CBS network. A-list guests of all generations were still queuing up to appear with him. Among those contributing cameos were Whitney Houston, Britney Spears, Justin Timberlake, Usher, Ricky Martin, Destiny's Child, Gloria Estefan and Guns N' Roses' Slash, as well as old-school superstars Ray Charles, Dionne Warwick, Liza Minnelli and Luther Vandross. Britney's duet with Michael on 'The Way You Make Me Feel' was a highlight of the shows, but she was distressed when it failed to make the TV edit. Legendary actor Marlon Brando, then aged 77, gave a curious, largely incoherent tribute speech – that too was cut from the television showing. Yet the biggest emotional home run of the event came when Michael reunited with his brothers on stage for the first time since the mid-eighties, the Jacksons on fire as they ran through a medley of their hits.

As America and the world were plunged into shock by the terrorist attacks of 9/11, it was rather inventively reported that Michael had fled to a New Jersey "secure location" with current best friends Elizabeth Taylor and Brando. However, he soon organized a benefit concert for the victims – named United We Stand: What More Can I Give? – in Washington, D.C.

In February 2002, he stunned fans with a revelation of his own. He was a father for the third time. He presented son Prince Michael II, who he announced had been conceived via artificial insemination, but added that he'd had "a personal relationship" with the mystery mother. Later, he contradicted this, explaining that she was a surrogate, who he didn't know. The child became, rather unfortunately, known as "Blanket", and Michael didn't win any Father of the Year awards when, showing the infant off to eager fans, he dangled the baby from the railings of his hotel balcony in Berlin. As soon as he realized his over-enthusiastic error of judgement, he pulled the boy back, but the PR damage was done. "I got caught up in the excitement of the moment," he told the press, apologetically. "I would never intentionally endanger the lives of my children." Sadly, he'd undone much of the public image rehabilitation he'd been building. The *Independent on Sunday* opined, "The last decade of Michael Jackson's life has hardly been his most glorious phase, but the events of the last six months have seen him slide downwards at unprecedented speed. If Jackson was

Right All the hullaballoo around Michael meant people sometimes overlooked his sublime singing voice.

> **If you don't have the memory of being loved, you are condemned to search the world for something to fill you up.**

ever "The King of Pop", there seems little doubt that his crown has now been broken into pieces."

Could he spring back once again? It wasn't to be an easy ride: his Heal the World foundation had to deal with complex tax issues; *Forbes* labelled his career "a franchise in demise"; a concert promoter sued him over cancellations; *People* magazine called him a "loser". His finances were all but in meltdown. There were some moments of relief, as when Michael was best man at the wedding of old friend Liza Minnelli and David Gest, and a performance with rising star Beyoncé at the Radio Music Awards. There was also a birthday cake presentation at MTV's Video Music Awards. Yet even this turned sour when Britney Spears, presenting, mistakenly used the phrase "artist of the millennium" and a confused Michael gave a thank-you speech believing he'd just been awarded that title. And then things got really problematic for the beleaguered star.

In February 2003, the notorious Martin Bashir documentary *Living With Michael Jackson* ran on ITV in Britain, and ABC in the States. Jackson had been introduced to Bashir by his friend Uri Geller and had hoped the show would present him in a good light. Bashir, who'd shot to fame with his Princess Diana interview, did not do this. Granted "unfettered access" to Neverland, for months with his camera crew, the film-maker revealed Jackson admitting to "sleepovers" with young boys. "Why can't you share your bed?" Jackson said to the startled interviewer. "That's the most loving thing to do, to share your bed with someone." On top of this, there was further bile directed at his father, and an implausible claim that he'd only ever had two operations on his nose. There

was footage of flamboyant shopping sprees too. But the real problem for most viewers was the not-exactly-conventional closeness with much younger boys.

Jackson complained of an editorial stitch-up, but there was a fresh avalanche of opprobrium. Before long, he was arrested on suspicion of molesting a 12-year-old cancer survivor, a frequent Neverland guest, Gavin Arvizo. The singer posted $3 million bail, but then had to wait until 2005 for the case to go to trial. The media mugged it up with a tasteless circus-style framing, comparable in some ways to the O. J. Simpson court fiasco. Michael didn't behave wisely, either, naively waving and smiling at supportive fans outside the courtroom, leaping up on top of cars. The trial lasted four months, cost a fortune, and Jackson was acquitted of all charges. Yet his image and reputation were undoubtedly tarnished; some might say trashed. His financial troubles multiplied. His already fragile psyche had taken a battering. He had to sell off stakes in Neverland and, a figure of suspicion and loathing to many, take leave of the United States.

He roamed between Bahrain – initially a guest of the ruler's son, who he then fell out with him over a stalled music/book contract – and the UK and Ireland, among other stop-offs. His sister La Toya Jackson, told the press, "Michael hasn't been back to Neverland since the trial. He never wants to see it again." (It had been turned upside down by investigators.) "The memories now are so awful." It wasn't until 2006 that Michael felt healed enough to appear in public again, when he arrived at the Guinness World Records office in London to accept multiple awards. His album releases were now invariably repackaged hits compilations. He did emerge Stateside, though, for James Brown's funeral. A premature attempt to hit the stage again was not a triumph when, at the 2006 World Music Awards in London, he arrived two hours late, semi-sang a section of 'We Are The World', blew kisses instead of properly performing, and generally looked as bewildered as the audience. Beyoncé confirmed she'd had to persuade a highly nervous Michael to leave

Opposite Not the happiest of days: arriving at court in Santa Maria, 2005.

Below What his fans loved him for. Their support was loyal.

his dressing room. "He didn't want to come out," she said, and nobody was especially surprised to hear it.

It had been a gruelling and demoralising period both for Jackson and for his fans, all of whom wondered if some good news would ever arrive. In March 2009, it seemed it had, and supporters' loyalty was rewarded with – for a few months at least – some cause for jubilation.

Thousands of fans and hundreds of reporters assembled at London's O2 Arena on 25 March for a very special announcement. There was already hysterical excitement in the air when, naturally ninety minutes late, Michael Jackson took to the stage to reveal that he was set to play his first full live shows for eight years. He announced a full resident season of concerts, dubbed "This Is It", from 9 July onwards. Originally, he declared ten shows, but demand was so high that this figure was soon increased to an astonishing fifty, running from July through to early 2010 and thus shattering the previous record, held by Prince, of twenty-one nights at the venue. It was to be the comeback of the new century. But they were always planned as Michael's final flurry. This was it.

"This is it," said Michael, smiling. "I just want to say these will be my final show performances in London. When I say this is it, I really mean this is it. I'll be performing the songs my fans want to hear. This is really it, the final curtain call. I love you, I really do. You have to know that. From the bottom of my heart. This is it! I'll see you in July!" The promoters, AEG, described it as "history in the making – as King of Pop Michael Jackson performs in London for the last time. Long may he reign!" The press ran stories declaring that this would boost London's economy as people travelled from across the world to see their hero, and mused on whether a farewell world tour might follow.

Others weren't quite so positive. Some even suggested that the Michael at the press conference was a double, an imposter. They questioned his health and fitness,

Opposite Bouncing back. Kneepads come recommended when jumping this high.

Above In rehearsals for the planned This Is It comeback dates Michael looked fit and energized.

asking with some justification – with hindsight – whether the thin-looking 50-year-old would be up to such a heavy schedule of shows. Fans believed, of course, and tickets were soon being touted for thousands of dollars. Michael was seen house-hunting in the UK with his three children, and fitness training in LA. The promoters felt pushed to announce that Jackson was "in tremendous condition, after a battery of tests". One thing was undisputed: everybody was talking about Michael Jackson again. The anticipation was such that this felt as if it would be one of the all-time great pop spectacles. Any lingering ill feeling from the court cases and scandals had almost been blown away by a fresh wave of enthusiasm, and a reminder of Jackson's huge global popularity.

Rehearsals at the Staples Center in LA were lengthy and largely fruitful, and footage seen since has shown that Michael still had magic in his voice and his dancing feet. There was what seemed to be a glitch when the first dates were pushed back a few days later in July, with perfectionism and stage logistics being cited as an excuse. But as the countdown ticked, on 25 June came dreadfully sad news that crushed the euphoria and replaced it with tragedy.

It was Thursday, 25 June when Michael Jackson's death was announced. It was reported that he'd suffered a heart attack at his rented house in Holmby Hills, off Sunset Boulevard in LA. He had apparently collapsed and stopped breathing after an excess of Demerol, a powerful painkiller. Emergency services were called and paramedics fought to save him. An ambulance rushed him to UCLA Medical Center, where further attempts to revive and resuscitate him were unsuccessful. Michael's mother and some family members raced to the hospital, as did Elizabeth Taylor, and aghast fans, hoping against hope, gathered outside. The media did their best, for once, to eschew random speculation and stick to facts. The sad fact was that Jackson's death from heart failure was confirmed by the LA county coroner at 2.26 p.m.

The world was pitched into a state of shock; the unexpectedness of this turn of events all the sharper given the optimism of the recent comeback announcements. Michael's "strange and brilliant" life and career were eulogized across the planet, from Hollywood to Indiana, from Paris to Glastonbury. The TV and radio news channels pretty much devoted themselves to the subject, 24/7, for days on end. "The day the music died," one fan wept on camera, speaking for many. Just as in Michael's life, there was a contrast between the respect shown for his musical gifts – his songs and videos ran everywhere, acclaimed and loved – and the prurient snooping into his off-stage life. Soon the focus moved on to the blame game, with Jackson's doctor targeted. The Jackson family demanded investigations and a second autopsy. The conspiracy theories ran riot, with the craziest positing that the star had faked his death, either to drum up publicity or to avoid the imminent live shows. Inevitably, the less than rigorous *National Enquirer* had a "Jacko Alive" picture on its pages within days.

It sank in, however, that the King of Pop was dead. Dignity was afforded his musical achievements and cultural impact. *Time* magazine hailed "the way he blended black music and white". Others used the word "genius". Thoughtful pieces analysed the divisions between the artist and the celebrity, the latter the "Frankenstein's monster" fuelled by elective surgery. Mostly, we all mourned our memories of the three main phases of Michael: the buoyant, joyful talent of the Jackson 5 years, the all-conquering, pioneering superstar of the eighties, and the compelling and

Above Happier times with President Bill Clinton.

Opposite above A saddening memento of Michael's arrest.

Opposite below Jackson is pictured smiling during rehearsals at the Staples Center in Los Angeles in 2009. He passed away just two days later.

Santa Barbara County Sheriff's Dept.

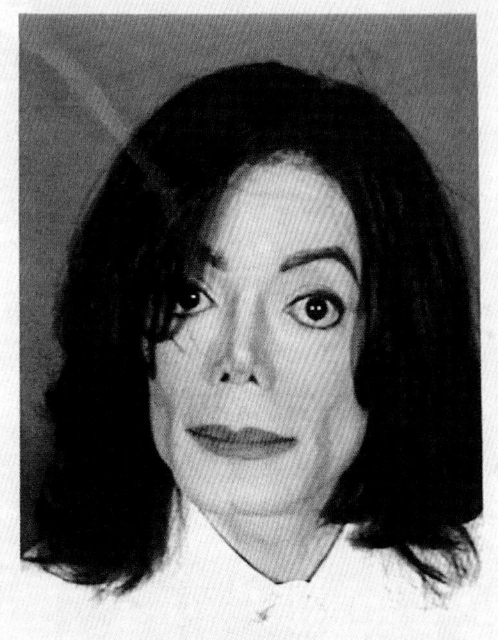

11/20/2003
Photo Image of:
NAME: JACKSON, MICHAEL
RAC: B SEX: M
DOB: 8/29/1958 AGE: 45
HGT: 511 WGT: 120
BLD: CMP:
HAI: BLK EYE: BRO
MKS:
BOOKING #: 621785

Michael Jackson
Thriller
WE LOVE YOU
FOREVER

“ This is such a tragic loss and a terrible day. Michael Jackson has made a bigger impact than any other artist in the history of music.

curious “Wacko Jacko” character. As one critic noted, it had never been easy to imagine this Peter Pan persona, in many ways an eternal child, embracing old age. Happier for us all is to recall Jackson in his heyday, his fluid body moving full of flame, his voice pirouetting with ecstasy and yearning.

Famous friends were quick to pay tribute. “This is such a tragic loss and a terrible day,” said Beyoncé. “Michael Jackson has made a bigger impact than any other artist in the history of music. He was magic. He was what we all strive to be. He will always be the King of Pop.” “An extraordinary child touched by ability,” said Cher. “He could sing like nobody else.” “An inspiration... I'm devastated,” said Britney Spears, while Madonna offered, “I can't stop crying over the sad news. The world has lost one of its greats, but his music will live on forever.” Ex-wife Lisa-Marie Presley brought a personal touch: “I am so very sad and confused with every emotion possible. I am heartbroken for his children, who I know were everything to him, and for his family. This is such a massive loss on so many levels.”

As the media worked itself into a frenzy of gossip and guesswork, helped by the drug-use element of the tragedy, it emerged that Jackson's will left his estate to his mother and his children. Katharine Jackson (but not Joseph) was to be his children's guardian, with Diana Ross named as back-up choice. Debbie Rowe was said to be displeased. Rumours abounded about the financial implications of the cancelled concert dates. Eventually, the *This Is It* film and album came out, showing – at least in flashes – that the return of pop's royalty would have been no disappointment, his talent still brightly there. Other posthumous albums of remixes and previously unreleased material in the

Previous pages: Left Devastated fans pay their respects at a hastily erected shrine in tribute to their hero. **Right** A pensive King of Pop.

Opposite A more mature Michael Jackson, gazing reflectively.

Above The face had changed; the generational talent remained.

Following pages This tribute wall in Los Angeles was just one of many erected around the world – a tribute to Michael's legacy.

MICHAEL JACKSON
AUGUST 29, 1958 - JUNE 25, 2009

"YOU ROCK MY WORLD"
RIP Michael Love Garcia Fam
R.I.P MJ
THANKS MJ
I Love You
THE KING!!
I Love So Much
Michael
Paul
2009

years since have been of mixed merit. The Jackson name's earnings have, however, increased. There have been stage productions based on Michael's songs, an epic touring Cirque du Soleil extravaganza, and a thoughtful documentary by director Spike Lee.

Back in July 2009, the Michael Jackson memorial service was in itself a globally watched phenomenon. The now-united Jackson family wore dark glasses; the brothers wore one diamante glove each in their shining light's honour. After a private ceremony at the Forest Lawn memorial park, Michael's gold casket, draped in red roses, arrived by motorcade at the Staples Center, where the This Is It concert rehearsals had been running. Now pure glitzy showbiz took over, and you can't argue against that being what he would've wanted. In front of a packed house and a gargantuan television audience, what followed was part-funeral, part-tribute concert, part-celebration. With the coffin nestling at the front of the stage, the songs and eulogies came with a mix of genuine and ostentatious emotion. Smokey Robinson read messages, Mariah Carey, Lionel Richie and Stevie Wonder sang and Berry Gordy Jr called Michael "the greatest entertainer that ever lived". There were more songs, from Jennifer Hudson and Usher, and Jermaine Jackson, who performed Charlie Chaplin's 'Smile' after Brooke Shields announced it as Michael's favourite. The Rev. Al Sharpton attested that Michael "broke down the colour curtain. He put us on the cover of magazines and TV. He made us love each other." He also credited President Obama's election win to Michael, but, in context, you can forgive the over-reaching. More poignantly, Sharpton looked at Jackson's children, saying, "Wasn't nothing strange about your daddy. What was strange was what your daddy had to deal with."

Michael Jackson's life was certainly unusual, but in his greatest, healthiest, happiest years, he'd brought something of wonder and miracle back to music. Ten years on from his premature passing, and we still thrill to those peerless pinnacles of pop.

Below Fans created tributes to their tragically departed hero.

Right Still in the limelight: A holographic image of Michael Jackson performs onstage during the 2014 Billboard Music Awards.

Michael Jackson
MJ

“He brought something of miracle and wonder back to music. Ten years on from his premature passing, we still thrill to those peerless pinnacles of pop...

MU

ALBUM B

SIC

Y ALBUM

GOT TO BE THERE (1972)

It wasn't certified gold until August 2013, but *Got To Be There* has now sold close to a million copies in the USA, and well over three million worldwide. Back in 1972, Michael's sweet, smiling debut was best recognized for his first two solo singles: that majestic title ballad and the contrastingly jolly and breakneck-paced follow-up 'Rockin' Robin'. In the UK, his unforgettable version of Bill Withers' 'Ain't No Sunshine' was also released as a hit single, while Stateside, the Leon Ware composition 'I Wanna Be Where You Are' was chosen.

The album announced, to the surprise of few, that Michael was perfectly capable of thriving outside The Jackson 5, without his brothers. *Rolling Stone* declared it, "Slick, artful and every bit as good as the regular Jackson 5 product," noting his "touching voice" and "innocence and utter professionalism". It was, it concluded, "fascinating and ultimately irresistible." The debut went to number 14 on the *Billboard* pop Chart and number three on the R&B chart. (In the UK it made a disappointing number 37, but as pop stars were then more focused on hit singles, the word was nonetheless being plentifully spread about Michael's gifts.)

Convinced and determined that young Michael was a solo superstar in the making, Berry Gordy Jr called in almost every producer and songwriter in his impressive Motown contact book to support the project. At 14, Michael's voice was already changing, so in a way the album captures lightning in a bottle. As a rather hurried whole album, as a cohesive entity, it may not fully hang together, but the voice is special and its peak moments are stunning. The title track in itself sits beautifully among the very best work in Jackson's canon.

The album's cast list is testament to Gordy's pulling power, and the fact that already everybody wanted to work with the child prodigy. When your writing team includes Withers, Ware, Willie Hutch, Holland-Dozier-Holland and Carole King, and productions and arrangements come from Motown giants Hal Davis and The Corporation, you know you're in more than capable hands. Elliot Willensky had penned 'Got To Be There', produced by Hal Davis at Hitsville West in Hollywood, which had emerged as the launch single in October 1971. Hutch was in charge of vocal arrangements. It scored a number four *Billboard* hit, reaching number five in the UK.

New Jersey-born Willensky was never a household name, but he went on to write a 1986 duet for Michael's brother Jermaine and Whitney Houston ('If You Say My Eyes Are Beautiful'), and a 1999 Off-Broadway musical called *Abby's Song*. His main job was as musical coordinator for the then popular CBS TV variety show, *Tony Orlando and Dawn* (who enjoyed their own catalogue of hits). Interestingly, he'd been a research scientist in his youth, but science's loss was music's gain. The many cover versions of 'Got To Be There' (by, for example, Chaka Khan, George Benson, The Miracles and Boys II Men) presumably kept him comfortably off financially. He died in 2010, aged 66.

'Rockin' Robin' had been a top two rock 'n' roll hit for Bobby Day as far back as 1958. It was written by the veteran composer Leon Rene, whose songs had been performed by The Inkspots and Glenn Miller, under the pseudonym Jimmie Thomas. For Michael, it surpassed even 'Got To Be There' in chart positions, racing to number one on the *Cashbox* chart and number two in *Billboard*. Yet if the album has a pinnacle of passion to rival 'Got To Be There', it's 'Ain't No Sunshine'.

This Bill Withers classic had only recently emerged on Withers' own 1971 album *Just As I Am*, produced in Memphis by Booker T. Jones. His original featured a superb playing team of wall-to-wall legends, with Donald 'Duck' Dunn on bass, Al Jackson Jr on drums and one Stephen Stills on guitar. Its rise into the Top Ten and a gold disc for Withers explained the decision not to release it as a single for Michael in his homeland, but Britain was at that point slightly less familiar with Bill's work. It presumably remained unknown to Jackson (and perhaps Gordy too) that Withers had been inspired to write the song when watching a film about alcoholism: 1962's *Days of Wine and Roses*, directed by Blake Edwards and starring Jack Lemmon and Lee Remick. Discussing these characters' influence on the song's lyrics, Withers explained, "They were both alcoholics who were alternately weak and strong. It's like going back for seconds... on rat poison. Sometimes you miss things that aren't particularly good for you. That's what crossed my mind, watching that movie..." Yet it's safe to guess Michael sang purely of pining for a loved one, such is the innocent, affecting emotion of his rendition. As for the multiple repetitions of "I know, I know", Withers had first intended these as a stop gap until he wrote some "better" lyrics. The more experienced musicians he was then working with told him not to change it, that it just worked. Pop poetry by accident. Bill was just happy he wasn't still making toilet seats for aeroplanes; the unglamorous job he'd had when writing it.

'I Wanna Be Where You Are' was created by Arthur "T-Boy" Ross (Diana Ross's younger brother) and Leon Ware, who among other fine achievements went on to co-write and co-produce Marvin Gaye's *I Want You* album. It gave Michael his third straight Top Ten hit, right off the bat. It was the first-ever collaboration between Ware and Ross, and quietly became one of the most covered Jackson hits, with Marvin Gaye and The Fugees among those to later record versions. Dusty Springfield performed the song on Lulu's BBC TV show, and it was sampled in subsequent decades by Jennifer Lopez, 50 Cent and Chris Brown. Yet perhaps the highest profile post-Jackson interpretation came from Beyoncé, who performed it on tour many times. In 2011, at the Michael Forever tribute concert in Cardiff, she said before starting the number, "I remember seeing Michael Jackson for the first time. Lord knows I fell in love. Watching him, I realized exactly what I wanted to be. He inspired me so much. As a matter of fact this was the first song I performed with Destiny's Child... it's the song we auditioned to get our record deal. It was the beginning of our future. I love you forever Michael Jackson."

Among the other stand-outs on *Got To Be There* was Michael's version of the 1967 Supremes classic chart-topper 'Love Is Here And Now You're Gone', one of Holland-Dozier-Holland's most underrated and poignant works of beauty. As the B-side of 'Rockin' Robin', Michael's rendition perhaps never got the attention it deserved, but it's a tender reading of the dramatic break-up tale, and as a Diana Ross fan and friend, Michael gave a vocal display of respectful sincerity. The album closes with a cute cover of the Carole King standard 'You've Got A Friend', from her then-recent huge-selling album *Tapestry*. "The song was as close to pure inspiration as I've ever experienced," the revered King has said. "It wrote itself. It was written by something outside myself, through me."

Michael's debut album was re-mastered and reissued in 2009 as part of the triple box set, *Hello World: The Motown Solo Collection*, which compiled his first four solos. On its original release, however, *Got To Be There* introduced – and began to establish – Michael as an individual force. He was still one of The Jackson 5, but as many had already discerned he was too rich with talent to stay part of a team for much longer. He was saying hello to the world, and the world knew it had got to be wherever his voice was taking them.

RECORDED
June–November 1971

RELEASED
January 24, 1972

LABEL
Motown

PERSONNEL
Michael Jackson (vocals), The Corporation, Eddy Manson, James Anthony Carmichael, Gene Page, Dave Blumberg, plus various Motown musicians

PRODUCERS
Hal Davis, The Corporation, Willie Hutch

INITIAL CHART PERFORMANCES
US *Billboard* 100, No. 14; US *Billboard* R&B, No. 3; UK albums, No. 37

Above Michael's solo debut showed he could thrive outside The Jackson 5.

BEN (1972)

It's one of the strangest ballads of its era, but the song 'Ben' led Michael's second solo album to a higher American chart position than *Got To Be There*. It's sold five million copies, despite only yielding that one curiously themed single, which became Michael's first number one. It also won a Golden Globe and an Oscar nomination. Ben, it seemed, was a friend worth having, even if he was a rat.

Yes, a rat. 'Ben' – sometimes called 'Ben's Song' – was written for the 1972 horror film, a sequel to 1971's *Willard*. The movie's plot saw lonely boy Danny befriending Ben, the leader of Willard's trained colony of rats. Ben at first protects Danny (played by Lee Harcourt Montgomery) from bullying, and helps him cope with a heart ailment. But then things turn violent and gory, as Ben and the rats get murderous. They're eventually torched by police flame-throwers, but Ben escapes and flees to Danny, who tends to his wounds. Written by Gilbert Ralston and directed by Phil Karlson, the movie gathered a review from Roger Ebert, who pointed out, "The whole idea is to be disgusted because the actors have rats all over them." No *Citizen Kane* then, and it lacked even the star power of *Willard* (Ernest Borgnine, Elsa Lanchester). So it was fortunate indeed to carry the notable ballad, which has meant the film being remembered long after its artistic expiry date.

The song was performed by lead actor Montgomery (even younger than Jackson) within the film, and then by Jackson over the end credits. After it picked up the Golden Globe, there was optimism it would triumph at the 1973 Academy Awards, but despite Michael performing it at the ceremony in front of an illustrious audience, it was pipped to the prize by Maureen McGovern's 'The Morning After' from *The Poseidon Adventure*. Still, Michael enjoyed it reaching number one in the US pop chart for a week, as well as dominating the Australian charts with an eight-week run at the top.

While it's odd to think of a young boy singing a ballad to a rat, it perhaps helped to nurture Michael's love of animals not normally known as pets. And he very nearly didn't land the song at all – fellow early-age pop star, and subject of much puppy love, Donny, Osmond had been offered the number first. Donny however, was on tour at the time the recording session was needed. So Michael lucked into a big hit, and an ongoing oddball association with bizarre critters. He'd already become the youngest person to have a chart-topper when The Jackson 5's 'I Want You Back' had beaten all-comers in 1970. Now, at 14, he became the third youngest solo artist ever to achieve a similar feat. Not quite the youngest this time: Stevie Wonder had taken 'Fingertips' to number one when he was thirteen, and Donny Osmond himself had more recently done it with 'Go Away Little Girl' before his fourteenth birthday.

Michael remained fond of the song: it appeared on 1981's album *The Jacksons Live!* Right now, he was still a member of The Jackson 5. Yet Berry Gordy was rushing, and pushing him to record more before his voice changed to a deeper vibe. Gordy executive-produced, but hired six different producers, so it was a collection of tracks rather than an organic album, but its mix of pop, soul and R&B has much charm. 'Everybody's Somebody's Fool' was lined up as the second single, but never released as such. The reasons remain nebulous, but it's probable that the schedule of maintaining both the solo career and the Jackson 5 career got too hectic at the time. Thom Bell and Linda Creed penned 'People Make The World Go Round', and their gifts as songwriters (and producers) were gloriously demonstrated in later years as they played a major part in helping to create the "Philadelphia Soul" sound. The Motown collective The Corporation took credits again, and Gordy even took sole writing credits for the album's closing track 'You Can Cry On My Shoulder', which Brenda Holloway had recorded in the mid-sixties.

Elsewhere, there were lively cover versions. Stevie Wonder's 1968 hit 'Shoo-Be-Doo-Be-Doo-Da-Day' was tackled, and 'Everybody's Somebody's Fool' was previously known as a Lionel Hampton jazz number. 'What Goes Around Comes Around' had a faint melodic resemblance to The Delfonics' classic 'Didn't I (Blow Your Mind This Time)', which of course Thom Bell had co-written. 'We've Got A Good Thing Going' had already seen the light of day as a B-side to the second single from the *Got To Be There* album, and 'In Our Small Way' had actually already appeared on that album too – a cheeky act of repurposing by Berry Gordy. Incidentally, 'We've Got A Good Thing Going' had another life in 1981, when reggae singer Sugar Minott took a new version into the UK top five. Perhaps the best-known song of all was 'My Girl', as Michael cooed the beautiful and evergreen 1964 Temptations hit, co-written by Smokey Robinson. Michael and the team bring a bundle of energy to the song, tossing in some Jackson Brothers-style call-and-response and a likeable funk rhythm.

Opposite A song from a horror movie about a rat gave Michael an unlikely smash.

RECORDED
November 1971–February 1972

RELEASED
August 4, 1972

LABEL
Motown

PERSONNEL
Michael Jackson (vocals), The Corporation, Hal Davis, Mel Larson, plus various in-house Motown players

PRODUCERS
Hal Davis, The Corporation, Byhal Davis, Berry Gordy, Mel Larson, Jerry Marcellino, Bobby Taylor

INITIAL CHART PERFORMANCES
US *Billboard* 100, No. 5; US *Billboard* R&B, No. 4; UK albums, No. 17

With 'Ben' leading the way, the album – and of course that moving Oscars performance – lifted the young man's profile further, reaching number five on the *Billboard* chart and number 17 in the UK, where the single made a respectable number seven. The single was the first of Michael's thirteen Hot 100 chart-toppers, and the album proved to be a slow-burner in the UK as his fame grew, landing a silver disc in 1973. Reviews were cautious, but more warm than cold. It was noted that The Corporation were less dominant as a writing/production force than they often were, and for all the cover versions, the original material was praised, although most agreed there wasn't a moment to match the glories of the gorgeous *Got To Be There*. Overall, though, it was, according to *Rolling Stone*, "a much stronger album than the first". It was "a testament to his talent", suggested *Entertainment Weekly*, while correctly pointing out it would also be defined by its title track. Others remarked on the "surprising amount of feeling" in Michael's vocals. His voice was still more than capable of surprising, and as it was soon to change, there were – as ever with Michael Jackson – further surprises in store.

Right That's showbiz! Michael and siblings join Cher for a TV (pre-)history class.

MUSIC & ME (1973)

He may be pictured strumming an acoustic guitar on the cover – an unlikely candidate to be the next Bob Dylan – but Michael doesn't actually play any instruments on his third solo album. *Music & Me* was a slightly problematical record, with glimmers of confusion now setting in about where priorities lay for Motown. With The Jackson 5, enjoying a strong spell? Or with Michael, the rising wonder kid? Motown were hesitant to burn any bridges and thus hedged their bets, for now.

At 14, Michael was also beginning to feel a need to express himself creatively rather than just sing covers and songs chosen for him by Berry Gordy. He was still adapting to changes in his voice as he grew, and hearing work by labelmates like Stevie Wonder and Marvin Gaye gave him an insatiable urge to try something bolder. As yet, though, at such a tender age, he would have to bide his time. He wanted to write songs, but wasn't as accomplished at this stage as he would later prove to be. He made his frustrations clear to his father/manager Joe, and in due course the Motown contracts were ended. *Music & Me* nonetheless was in the vein of its two predecessors, with Michael singing a mix of soul standards and bespoke material.

It perhaps didn't grasp Michael's full focus, as he was undergoing a busy tour schedule, travelling the world with his brothers. Subsequently, promotion too was under par, and although it's now sold two million copies, its chart placings were patchy. It's the lowest-seller of Michael's career – though almost any other artist would give their right arm to sell two million! The issue at the centre of it stalling (relatively) was that there was no major hit single. 'With A Child's Heart', a Stevie Wonder song, did moderately if not spectacularly well in the US, and in the UK the title song and 'Morning Glow' were released to little fanfare. In other territories different tracks ('Happy', 'Too Young') were chosen as singles, and maybe this general indecision – or lack of an obvious sure-fire hit – contributed to the album's inability to really break big. ('Happy' became a UK single ten years later, to promote a greatest hits album.)

As The Jackson 5 had a mini-resurgence, with 'Dancing Machine' a crossover smash, Motown didn't put out another Michael album for two years. He recorded sufficient material, but the label sat on it, feeling the brothers now had superior momentum. Ridiculous as it might now seem, there were those who thought Michael had been just a flash in the pan.

Left Meet the parents: a tuxedoed Michael greets Joe and Katherine.

Above Joe Jackson was still a very hands-on manager.

Following pages: Left On the cusp of adulthood, Michael dives into his solo career. **Right** *Music And Me* was his last album without his brothers for two years.

His version of Stevie's 'With A Child's Heart' has an affecting poignancy. Wonder had released the song on his 1966 album *Up-Tight*, and as a B-side, but even Michael couldn't make it a major hit. It went to number 50 on the *Billboard* pop chart, number 14 on the R&B chart, and number 23 on the Adult Contemporary chart – this last an indication of its efforts to be all things to all people. Amusingly, in a moment of light relief in that fateful and controversial TV interview with Martin Bashir in 2003, Michael confessed that not only could he not remember the song's lyrics, he actually had no recollection of the song's recording at all.

Michael was joined by Marlon and Jackie Jackson for backing vocals on the title track, while 'Too Young' was the enduring ballad made famous by Nat King Cole in 1951. Interestingly, Donny Osmond had enjoyed a UK number one with it a year prior to Michael's recording, so one wonders if there was a competitive rivalry between the two young stars or whether someone at Motown figured that if fans liked Donny singing it, they'd love to hear Michael making it his own. Then again, maybe Michael was a fan of the 1960 Sam Cooke version.

'Happy' was a kind of sleeper hit, as addressed above, and bears a mind-blowingly prestigious writing team of Smokey Robinson and Michel Legrand. It was conceived as 'Love Theme From *Lady Sings the Blues*', though it never featured in the Diana Ross movie, a film Michael doubtless loved given the bravura starring performance by his friend and mentor. He often cited this as one of his favourite songs. Smokey himself later recorded it for his sublime *Quiet Storm* album. He'd been inspired by Legrand's melody. (The French composer is revered for his French Nouvelle Vague scores, and classic songs such as 'The Windmills Of Your Mind'.) "I was looking at the film and thought that was such a beautiful melody that I wanted to write some words for it," explained Smokey. "I went and sang them for Berry Gordy. He was really upset because I hadn't written them before the movie finished, so they couldn't be in the movie."

The album's producer was again Hal Davis, the Jackson 5's go-to guy and a man who wrote and produced for Motown for the best part of three decades. Not to be confused with Hal David – Burt Bacharach's brilliant regular lyricist – Davis had discovered Brenda Holloway, helped the young Stevie Wonder find his sound, and sprinkled his magic on Jackson 5 hits like 'I'll Be There' and – to show he moved with the times – 'Dancing Machine'. Michael must have been familiar with his recording techniques by now. Davis went on to produce such moments of magic as Diana Ross' 'Love Hangover', Thelma Houston's 'Don't Leave Me This Way' and classics for Eddie Kendricks and Gladys Knight. One would guess that while Michael would have been excited to record songs like 'Euphoria' – another Leon Ware composition – during these sessions, then taking on a Jerome Kern–Oscar Hammerstein show tune like 'All The Things You Are' (from a 1939 musical, *Very Warm For May*), might have been more of a Berry Gordy suggestion, testing the waters to see if the young star could thrive in other areas and markets. Even jazz artists famously declare this a tricky song to play (Charlie Parker and Chet Baker were among those who'd got to grips with it), so it's a credit to young Michael's voice that he not only handled it but made his unlikely version work.

Touring and appearing on TV with The Jackson 5 now dominated his diary, and there was a hiatus from solo releases. His voice would break, but his determination wouldn't. There would be one more album for Motown before Michael's music would really reveal his inner me.

Opposite Michael and brother Randy play with a boomerang while on tour in Australia, 1973.

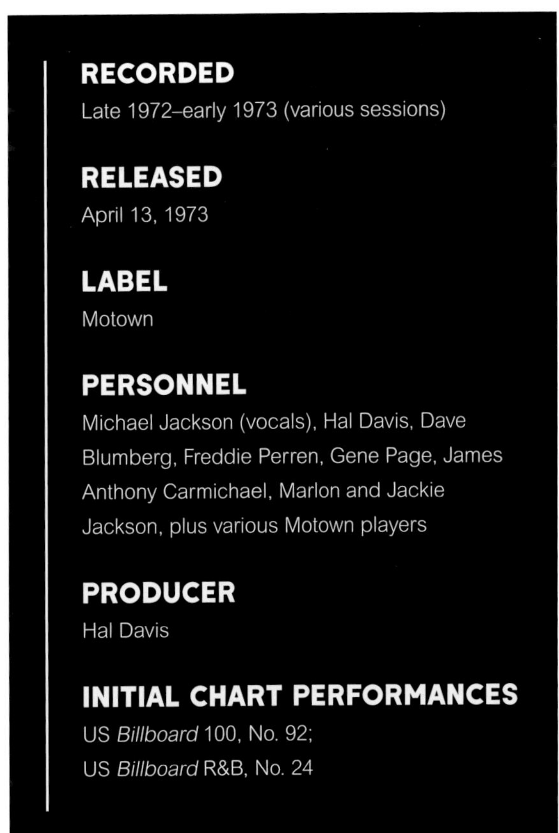

RECORDED
Late 1972–early 1973 (various sessions)

RELEASED
April 13, 1973

LABEL
Motown

PERSONNEL
Michael Jackson (vocals), Hal Davis, Dave Blumberg, Freddie Perren, Gene Page, James Anthony Carmichael, Marlon and Jackie Jackson, plus various Motown players

PRODUCER
Hal Davis

INITIAL CHART PERFORMANCES
US *Billboard* 100, No. 92;
US *Billboard* R&B, No. 24

FOREVER, MICHAEL (1975)

Two years on from *Music & Me* came Michael's fourth and final Motown studio album. At 16, his voice had evolved and the songs had a more mature overall feel, but the record company failed to realize that The Jackson 5's massive hit with 'Dancing Machine' marked a watershed in what the public wanted and expected from its Jackson boys. Contemporary dance music, the midwife to disco, was booming, and Michael should probably have been ushered in that direction. Evidently – as his next, game-changing album was to prove – he was becoming aware of that himself. It was no coincidence that a year later he and his brothers (except for Jermaine) parted ways with Motown and moved to CBS/Epic Records.

Most of the album had been recorded in 1974, but the snowballing success of 'Dancing Machine' kept Michael and those around him hectically busy, so the release was held until January 1975. It wasn't a hit internationally, and its US chart showings were modest, though it has now passed the one million sales mark. A short album whose ten songs barely run over a half-hour in total, it's not the record that makes Michael remembered forever. In its hints of smooth soul and polite rhythms however, one can – if one squints hard – discern in spells the first mild shifts towards a more youthful, dance-floor-orientated sound.

While one can criticize the album for lacking true inspiration, it's a pleasure to hear Michael's voice moving into its next phase, and the production and writing team was loaded with class acts. Hal Davis was involved again, but shared duties with Motown demi-gods Eddie Holland Jr and Brian Holland, among others. It's a quirk of chronology that the biggest hit single from the album – 'One Day In Your Life' – wasn't actually released until 1981.

Instead, the singles chosen contemporaneously were "We're Almost There" and "Just A Little Bit Of You", both written by the Holland Brothers (sans Dozier). They'd been commissioned to create numbers that Michael's now lower voice would enjoy. The former, produced by Brian, crept to a disappointing no. 54 on the *Billboard* Hot 100, while the latter, with arrangements by James Anthony Carmichael, made a healthier number 23 on

Above No matter what the setting, Michael delivered electric performances.

Right We're almost there: with each release he was getting closer to megastardom.

RECORDED
Across 1974 (various sessions)

RELEASED
January 16, 1975

LABEL
Motown

PERSONNEL
Michael Jackson (vocals), David Blumberg (arrangements), LT Horn (engineering, mixing), Arthur G. Wright (arrangements), Eddy Manson (arrangements), Freddie Perren (arrangements), Sam Brown III (arrangements), plus various Motown musicians.

PRODUCERS
Eddie Holland Jr., Brian Holland, Hal Davis, Freddie Perren, Sam Brown III

INITIAL CHART PERFORMANCES
US *Billboard* 200, No.101;
US *Billboard* R&B, No. 10

the US Pop singles chart, and number 4 on the Soul chart, giving Jackson his biggest solo hit in three years.

Of course a popular post-script came six years later when Motown released the previously unheralded 'One Day In Your Life' as they put together a compilation album of the same name to cash in on Michael's booming new phase of success with Epic. (That album went on to sell two million, so bright was Michael's star now). Even with Michael's status, nobody quite expected the sweet yearning ballad, beautifully sung, to become a British chart-topper, but it was the sixth best-seller of that year in the UK. Composed by Sam Brown III and Renee Armand, its minor presence in the US made its UK triumph one of those enjoyable mysteries that occasionally baffle pop experts and record company focus groups. (It also went to number one in Ireland and the Netherlands).

Elliot Willensky, who'd authored Michael's solo breakthrough 'Got To Be There', made a reappearance,

Left Sister act: with a young Janet and brother Randy.

Opposite Michael and Donny Osmond were two of the leading teen pin-ups of the era.

co-writing 'We've Got Forever' with Mack David, and the curiously pitched 'Dear Michael' with Hal Davis. 'Cinderella Stay Awhile' and 'Dapper-Dan', if not home runs, at least lyrically attempted something more interesting than generic pop platitudes. All these songs were later included on the previously mentioned September 2009 collection of Michael's early work, *Hello World*, which contrary to some reports was planned and announced before, not after, Michael's death that summer.

As the only album by Michael that doesn't share its title with a song therein, *Forever, Michael* was paradoxically a sign that he wasn't going to stay in the same musical modes forever. The musical arrangements, classy as they were, felt more fitted to one of the older, even more established acts on Motown, and like his brothers Michael was eager to try new sounds and styles. Their Motown days, glorious as they had in the most part been, were done. As was Michael's own unorthodox approximation of a childhood. It would be wrong to say that nobody envisaged him graduating from child star to major global star in adulthood, but those that did were arguably outnumbered by sceptics. Yet, Michael Jackson was, within four years, to conjure up an epic and electrifying evolution.

"Michael was eager to try new sounds and styles. The Motown days, glorious as they had mostly been, were done.

OFF THE WALL (1979)

"The argument for Michael Jackson's greatness in the recording studio," wrote Nelson George a quarter-century after the release of *Off The Wall*, "begins with his arrangements of 'Don't Stop 'Til You Get Enough'. The layers of percussion and the stacks of backing vocals, both artfully choreographed to create drama and ecstasy on the dance floor, still rock parties in the 21st century." It may well rock parties into the 22nd. *Off The Wall* was Michael's new beginning; its place in music history is now confirmed.

"There is no way of preparing for success," said Quincy Jones. "Especially when it's the biggest success that ever occurred in music." Yet in a way Michael had prepared. He'd stopped releasing stop-gap, sub-standard solo albums. As the seventies roared towards the eighties, he'd grown up. The Jacksons had severed their latterly traumatic ties with Motown, and established a thriving group career with hits like 'Shake Your Body (Down To The Ground)', sung and co-written by Michael. Although his detour into the world of film with *The Wiz* had stuttered, he had, crucially, met producer Quincy Jones on that venture. While in New York, he'd visited Studio 54 and other nightclubs, and soaked up the prevalent sounds. His grasp of the current, coupled with Quincy's vast experience, from Sinatra to Aretha, made for a golden ticket.

Michael thought of this as his first "proper" solo album; his first as a "grown man". They sat down and discussed what they wanted, he said, and it all turned out "exactly as we planned". Quincy wasn't without his doubts at first, but the team they assembled was dazzling. Contributing songwriters included Paul McCartney and Stevie Wonder, while the secret weapon was the then little-known maestro from Cleethorpes, Rod Temperton, of British dance group Heatwave, who brought three to-be-timeless tunes. Jackson's own writing contributions were dynamite. He was initially modest about this aspect to his game. "I feel guilty having to put my name on the songs I write," he laughed disarmingly. "I do write and compose them, and I do the scoring, lyrics, and melodies. But still it's a... it's a work of God!"

Sessions ran between the tail end of 1978 and June 1979 in several Los Angeles studios, most notably Westlake. They took risks, as when Temperton presented his three songs ('Off The Wall', 'Rock With You', 'Burn This Disco Out'), thinking they'd choose their favourite. Michael fell in love with all three, and nailed the vocals for them all in two inspired sessions. He'd stay up late to learn the lyrics off by heart, believing he could get wrapped up in them

Opposite Michael thought of *Off The Wall* as his first "proper" solo album.

Below Award time – Bonnie Pointer, Michael and La Toya Jackson at the American Music Awards.

RECORDED
December 1978–June 1979

RELEASED
August 10, 1979

LABEL
Epic

PERSONNEL
Michael Jackson (vocals, arrangements), Patti Austin (vocals), Quincy Jones (arrangements), Johnny Mandel (string arrangements), Rod Temperton (arrangements), Stevie Wonder (rhythm arrangement), Ben Wright (string arrangements), Tom Bahler (rhythm arrangement, vocal arrangement), plus various session singers and musicians

PRODUCERS
Quincy Jones, Michael Jackson

INITIAL CHART PERFORMANCES
US *Billboard* No. 3; UK album charts No. 3

better – inhabit them fully – if he wasn't stealing glances at a lyric sheet. His whole body would take a role in a vocal, moving and feeling it from head to toe. Temperton, smartly, had done his homework beforehand and written to suit Michael's punchy, powerful technique.

It's the first "Oooh!" of *Off The Wall* that sets the exhilarating tone, as 'Don't Stop 'Til You Get Enough', allegedly penned by Michael in his kitchen, starts turning up the heat. Its euphoric mix of (Bee Gees-inspired) disco rhythms and his urgent, now unrestrained whoops, grunts and yelps gave us, unapologetically and proudly, the new adult Jackson. If his mother was nervous it was all rather "suggestive", Quincy knew enough to encourage him not to hold back. He pointed out that at Motown everybody had mostly sung in a high register, but he wanted to feel Michael's full range, taking on "mature" themes. It felt as if Michael was channelling Al Green, James Brown, Sam Cooke, Sly Stone and Marvin Gaye, yet coaxing out something bold, new and previously untried. Jones' delicious wrapping of luxurious strings around the beat

Above Dancefloor king Michael with fellow star Donna Summer in 1982.

Right Longtime friend and mentor Diana Ross congratulates Michael on another trophy haul.

gave an extra gloss and, yes, shook your body. 'Rock With You' was just as fluid and irresistible, and proved influential to the point of absurdity on later stars such as Pharrell Williams and Justin Timberlake. 'Off The Wall' itself psalms the happy hedonism of the disco revolution as perfectly as, say, Sister Sledge's 'Lost In Music', as Michael sings, "Leave your nine to five up on the shelf, and just enjoy yourself."

Michael also wrote the fiery 'Workin' Day And Night', which he and Quincy, becoming obsessed with the project, were. McCartney's 'Girlfriend' is tame by comparison, but the Tom Bahler ballad 'She's Out Of My Life' is anything but a soppy sentimental interlude. It's given pathos and grit by Michael's breathtaking vocal performance, in which he seems – and is – on the very brink of real tears. Quincy had planned to bring that song to Sinatra, but felt now that Michael could tackle genuine, raw emotion. "And he cried on every take we did," he revealed. "I left the tears on the record – it was so real." For some, it became Michael's own 'My Way'. There were rumours it was dedicated to Tatum O'Neal, the young actress who'd been thought to be a girlfriend. Just a friendship, he asserted. In fact, of late, the "grown-up" Jackson had been photographed hitting Studio 54 with an eclectic crowd, including Liza Minnelli, Bianca Jagger, Woody Allen and Aerosmith's Steven Tyler.

Released in August 1979, *Off The Wall* was an unqualified success on every level. It tied a bow on the decade that was ending, and announced that there was a new white-hot star on the block. It took the best of that decade and injected it with the promise of the next. Its party of styles and sounds, rhythms and pleas, coalesced into a blueprint for everything this "mature" Michael could bring. It also declared that if he was big now, he was going to get even bigger. Its statistics were stunning: the first solo album to emit four US number one singles, it went eight times platinum there.

Twenty million sales followed worldwide, two million in the UK, and the industry lost count of the number of walls over which Michael was vaulting. That sleeve image too became iconic, as Michael beamed at the camera, wearing a tuxedo and white socks, the latter a trademark in waiting. His manager happily admitted that the tuxedo was the team's idea, but "the socks were his".

The world was left reeling by the confidence and charm of the album. It felt as if Michael had fully rediscovered the joy of singing that he'd first displayed as a boy. Reviewers hailed his unmatched vocal ability; others compared his transition from teenage star to adult genius to that of Stevie Wonder. At the American Music Awards, *Off The Wall* won Favourite Soul/R&B Album and Michael won Favourite Male Soul/R&B Artist, while 'Don't Stop...' took Favourite Soul/R&B Single. There were *Billboard* awards for Top Black Artist and Top Black Album, but just the one Grammy in 1980 – for Best Male R&B Vocal Performance. The perfectionist in Michael felt aggrieved. "It was totally unfair that it didn't get Record of the Year and it can never happen again," he complained. That year's other album-chart giants in

the US were Led Zeppelin, The Eagles, Supertramp, The Bee Gees and Donna Summer. In 2008, in a case of too little too late, the Grammys did induct the record into their Hall of Fame, but, in 1980, the singer was peeved and didn't care who knew it. "I wasn't too happy," he declared. "For the next album, I refuse to let them ignore me. I set my heart on it."

Well, that next album was set to be something else. The Jackson and Jones pairing was to make magic for a booming nine years. *Off The Wall*, however, will always be the one that established Michael as a star of electric talent and vibrant vision. It broke disco out across new terrain, and into new, colour-blind ears, forecasting some of the futures of dance music, and stands as a series of vocal performances bordering on the divine. Michael? He wanted to go further. He wanted more.

Above Epic achievements: the success of 'Dancing Machine' had given The Jackson 5 a career boost as they became The Jacksons.

THRILLER (1982)

The world's best-selling album was generally gleefully received, but one or two reviews stand out today for missing the mark to an almost heroic degree. The *New York Times* spoke of Quincy Jones' "slightly anonymous production," which "depersonalized his individuality", and thought Michael Jackson was a "sometimes too practised performer". The *Village Voice* called it "virtually a hits-plus-filler job". Somehow, *Thriller* overcame these curious exceptions to gather its momentum and became an unstoppable global phenomenon. At the end of the decade, the *Toronto Star* summed its impact up thus: "A masterwork whose commercial success has since overshadowed Jackson's artistic accomplishments, and that's a pity. It was a record for the times, brimming with breathless anticipation and a dread fear of the adult world, a brilliant fantasy that pumped with sexual heat, yet made room for serious reflection." It also, according to John Rockwell, helped to breach "the destructive barriers that spring up regularly between white and black music."

For Michael's part, his ambitions were limitless. He praised the "great team, a lot of talent, good ideas" but made no apologies for his brimming confidence. "I knew we could do anything. The success of *Thriller* transformed many of my dreams into reality." Its formidable 42 minutes shifted the goalposts on the field of popular music. Incredibly, it was put together relatively quickly. In late April 1982, Michael and Quincy reconvened to out-do *Off The Wall* in their favoured studio, Westlake Audio in Los Angeles. "I wanted to do an album where every song was like a hit record," the star emphasized. "Why are some songs called 'album songs'? Why can't every song be so great that people would want to buy it as a single?" He wanted it to be not twice but thrice as good as its predecessor. "It can't be just as good because that would be a let-down," he said. "We'll get it right. I'm a perfectionist. I strive. I'll work until I drop." Quincy at first tried to manage his expectations, pointing out the unpredictability of musical vogues and the random luck usually involved in popular sales. Yet he couldn't help but get caught up in Michael's drive and enthusiasm. The team selected their favourites from literally hundreds of submitted songs, arguing the case for their individual preferences. "We turned that album upside down," said Quincy. His studio engineer Bruce Swedien confirmed he'd never seen Jones so obsessed with a project. He told his team their mission was nothing less than to save the music industry. As a counter-balance, Jackson's lawyer and business head John Branca talked up Michael's contributions. He agreed that Quincy did a great job, but added, "If you listen to Michael's demos for 'Billie Jean' and 'Beat It', you'll realize he was actually the mastermind of those." Michael himself spoke of spending 18-hour days in the studio, sleeping on the couch, waking up the next day to continue mixing. Jones concurred that Jackson had an all-or-nothing approach.

For all the perfectionism, *Thriller* was finished in around six months, and released upon an only partially suspecting planet at the end of November, in time for Christmas. It had been previewed in mid-October with a conservative, not fully representative choice of first single, the Jackson-Paul McCartney duet 'The Girl Is Mine'. A pleasant enough mock duel over a girl, but hardly displaying the fresh fire of the album. Michael and Paul had become friends after Michael phoned the ex-Beatle on a previous Christmas Day; Paul at first thought it was a prankster. He was of course less amused in due course by Michael's unsentimental business moves.

Right Red alert: *Thriller* thrust its way to becoming the world's best-selling album.

RECORDED
April 14–November 8, 1982

RELEASED
November 30, 1982

LABEL
Epic

PERSONNEL
Michael Jackson (vocals, drum machine), Janet Jackson (vocals), La Toya Jackson (vocals), Paul McCartney (vocals), Quincey Jones (arrangements), Rod Temperton (synthesizers, arrangements), James Ingram (vocals, arrangements), Jerry Hey (string arrangements), Vincent Price (voice over), plus various session arrangers, singers and musicians

PRODUCERS
Quincy Jones, Michael Jackson

INITIAL CHART PERFORMANCES
US *Billboard* No. 1; UK album charts No. 1

“Michael wanted the recognition he felt Off The Wall had been unjustly denied. He got it – winning a record-breaking eight Grammys in 1984...

The album was still being mixed as 'The Girl Is Mine' gently warmed up listeners. Things weren't going as smoothly as hoped. One CBS executive described the first mix as "horrible", with Quincy asking for an extra ten days and wanting to start mixing again from scratch. "It was nerve-wracking," recalled the exec, "but he did it." And so *Thriller* made the festive season shops. But it took a while to get going, as hit single after hit single raised its profile. Indeed it didn't top the *Billboard* chart until February '83, but upon reaching the top it resolutely stayed there for an astonishing 37 weeks. And even after it dropped, it frequently bounced back to its natural number one position. The Top Ten hit single count climbed to an unprecedented seven, as the album often sold a million a week. (Over the next four years, it's estimated that Jackson earned over 700 million dollars.) Now all he wanted was the award-ceremony recognition that he felt *Off The Wall* had been unjustly denied. He got it – winning a record-breaking eight Grammys at the 1984 ceremony. It was telling, with regard to the album's eclectic

Left Feeling the groove: *Thriller* moved on from the innocent boyhood image.

Above *Thriller* played around with spooky horror movie imagery.

Following pages 'Billie Jean', the second single, really put rocket-launchers under the album.

inspirations, that he picked up trophies not just in the R&B category, but in both Pop and Rock too.

Thriller was and remains a stunning, genre-jumping creation, living up to its name. After 'The Girl Is Mine' met a lukewarm-to-fair reception, the album's jewels turned any premature assumptions on their heads. To the slick dance rhythms revved up on *Off The Wall* it added harder-edged dancefloor styles and slashes of hard rock. In theme and tone too, it was darker, edgier, opening up Michael's fascination with horror movies, the supernatural and the quivers and shivers of paranoia. *Village Voice* noted his departure from his boyhood image of innocence. His writing was blooming: as well as the red herring of the McCartney duet, he was involved in that department on the unimpeachable classics 'Billie Jean', 'Beat It' and 'Wanna Be Startin' Something'. He'd often write by singing his ideas into a nearby cassette recorder.

It was 'Billie Jean', the second single, which put rocket-launchers under the album. His videos now became must-see "events", and once the then-young channel MTV embraced his music the rise of both he and the channel were guaranteed. All the stress and labour – at one point Michael had bickered with Quincy and considered scrapping the whole thing – and high costs (over three quarters of a million dollars all in) now paid dividends. The musicians, as Quincy had brought in members of soft-rock giants Toto and many others, had delivered. Nowhere is this more evident than on the flawless groove and forward motion of 'Billie Jean'. Louis Johnson's bass line draws

Opposite A mountain of awards confirmed that Quincy was the ideal producer for Jackson.

Above Michael with (L to R) David Geffen, Liza Minnelli and Quincy Jones.

“It’s curious how [‘Billie Jean’] foreshadows Michael’s subsequent troubles with intense fame and celebrity, not to mention his own complex path to parenthood.

us in, and here Michael's instincts deserve credit, as he'd pleaded with Quincy to allow the extended, teasing intro. (Franz Ferdinand's Alex Kapranos was, decades later, to correctly call this "the best bass line ever written"). Jones' experience told him the song part needed to start sooner, yet Michael told him, "But that's the jelly! That's what makes me want to dance!" On reflection, Quincy concurred. "When Michael Jackson tells you that's what makes him want to dance, the rest of us have to shut up."

It's a strange lyric for such a famously upbeat song, dealing with a fixated fan-cum-stalker who'd broken into the grounds of Hayvenhurst. She insists Michael has fathered her child. Michael does not agree. "She says I am the one... but the kid is not my son." Quincy explained that Michael had told him: "'Billie Jean' was about a girl who climbed over his wall. He woke up one morning and she was just lying by the pool in her bathing suit. She'd just invaded the place. And he said she accused him of being the father of one of her twins... !" It's curious how the song foreshadows Michael's subsequent troubles with intense fame and celebrity, not to mention his own complex path to parenthood.

The song's video was more light-hearted, but showcased Michael's mercurial dance moves, the paving stones beneath his twinkling toes lighting up and glowing green for go. It's not flashy by later standards, but it's the performer who brings the magic and charisma. MTV knew a winner when it saw one, and was no longer a predominantly "white acts" station. (Unfounded rumours spread that the song was about Paula Abdul, who was said to be involved with one of Michael's brothers, and was soon to begin her own pop career. She'd later work closely with his sister, Janet, on her videos).

'Beat It' was also a landmark. The team wanted a rock track to entice the "white rock fan" demographic. Who better to provide shrieking guitar solos than Van

Opposite MTV recognised a winner in Michael Jackson.

Above "When Michael tells you that's what makes him want to dance, the rest of us have to shut up," decreed Quincy.

Halen's dextrous Eddie Van Halen? He didn't realize what a big deal he was getting into, perhaps because he received no fee for his session. "Everyone from the band was out of town, so I figured: Who's gonna know if I play on this kid's record? I didn't want nothing – I thought maybe Michael will give me dance lessons one day! According to my band and my manager I was a complete fool." Quincy had called him, and told him to just do his own thing. "So that's what he did. And he played his ass off." The *West Side Story* tributes and twists of 'Beat It' guided its memorable video, with Michael insisting it was about pacifism. "Nobody has to be the tough guy," he said. "You can walk away from a fight and still be a man." The track was so hot that during one playback the studio's speakers caught fire.

Even hotter was 'Wanna Be Startin' Something', which Michael had written some years earlier. His vocals are ablaze, and Jones comes into his own here, raising the sonic stakes as the funk builds to a climactic Swahili chant. He even got Michael to sing some overdubs through a lengthy cardboard cylinder tube. The album's also rich with tracks that grow on you irreversibly. The beauty of 'Human Nature' and its deft chorus is sly and subtle, coaxing one of Michael's most delicate vocals ever. Stevie Wonder's a big fan of the song. 'Lady In My Life' is another Rod Temperton ballad, while 'P.Y.T. (Pretty Young Thing)' is a passionate R&B track, written by Jones with James Ingram, which in some ways pre-empts the "Nu-Soul" tropes that emerged in later years.

Of course the theatrical, or should we say cinematic, centrepiece of the album is that show-stealing title track. Rod Temperton had originally sketched it out under titles such as 'Starlight' or 'Midnight Man', but 'Thriller' ultimately felt special. The sound effects – thunder, gales, creaking doors, creepy footsteps, howling dogs – bring the atmosphere into *Twilight Zone*/Hammer horror-film territory, and the late addition of fright-fest icon Vincent Price's narration clinched the scary-movie feel. Temperton had to quickly write Price's speech in a cab en route to the studio, after Quincy called him to let him know the new idea. He asked the driver to go once more around the block and park at the back of the studio so he could finish off. It's another indication that Quincy's network reaches everywhere – his wife knew Price. Vincent was done in two impeccable takes. He was later given a gold record. 'Thriller', the song, of course rose to legendary status itself after the million-dollar video, then the most expensive ever made, became the planet's hottest talking point. Directed by Jon Landis – whose *An American Werewolf in London* had wowed

Michael – and with striking make-up by Rick Baker, it premiered on TV in early December 1983 and lifted the album's sales to another stratosphere. Michael had asked Landis, "I want to turn into a monster. Can I do that?" Be careful what you wish for. "A guy goes out on a date and confesses to the girl that he's different. I wanted to transform into different things." One record label observer commented on Michael being all about "business and bigness. Every new venture has to be bigger than Disneyland." *Thriller*'s exhilarating brew of Hollywood, mock-horror, disco and delight was achieving it.

As he Moonwalked at the 1983 Motown 25th Anniversary show, Jackson was the biggest star alive. *Thriller* sold another million copies in the next week alone. Its eight Grammys meant the 1984 ceremony was fundamentally The Michael Jackson Show (and broke Paul Simon's 1970 record of seven). *Thriller* was now officially history's biggest-selling album, and spin-off merchandising grew a life of its own. Everyone from Frank Sinatra to the Rev. Jesse Jackson sang Michael's praises. He was invited to the White House by the Reagans; given a star on Hollywood's Walk of Fame. And he attributed all his success to his pet animals. The persona of "Wacko" Jacko began to take root here. But what an achievement *Thriller* was, often referred to in the eighties as "the pulse of America". Transcending colour and race, vaulting over musical genre barriers, Jackson's status was ascending to Elvis/Beatles levels. When *Thriller* at last dropped from number one to number two, it's said that Michael cried. It was "the late-20th century's pre-eminent pop icon," suggested one magazine. And so was he.

Previous pages Transcending colour and race and musical genres, *Thriller* was "the pulse of America".

Opposite Mooching around on the 'Billie Jean' video set.

Above Zombie nation: Michael unfazed by creepy creatures.

Following pages Those videos helped to define pop music in the eighties.

BAD (1987)

Thriller was one tough act to follow. Yet Michael Jackson was good enough to pull it off. *Bad* was superbad, a personal project in which Michael wrote nine of the eleven songs, while he and Quincy Jones honed and extended their consummate collaborative techniques and pushed his vocal idiosyncrasies to euphoric new heights. The music swam between genres, nailing the essence of each, and it was the first album ever to spawn five *Billboard* number ones. (That record wasn't to be matched until Katy Perry's *Teenage Dream* equalled it in 2010–11). *Bad* was all good, and confirmed Jackson's greatness.

While his fame was now pulling him left, right and centre, in the studio Michael kept a sharp focus. The *Bad* sessions ran between November 1986 to July 1987, and the album's release five years on from the all-conquering *Thriller* was a huge, news-dominating, global event. The video for the title track was directed by Martin Scorsese, lasted 17 minutes, cost two million dollars (back then a lot of money) and introduced us to the star's surprising new image. Based on the time-honoured leather-and-chains bad-boy mythology, its twist on *The Wild One* and *West Side Story* brought in the crotch-grabbing, falsetto-yelping version of Michael, which became so iconic that many parodied it over subsequent years. *Bad* stormed in at number one and, while it couldn't match *Thriller* for sales – nothing could – it easily became one of the music industry's biggest-ever successes. His accompanying tour broke records, and each richly riveting hit single soundtracked most people's lives.

While that image reinvented him as a more aggressive, punkier, dirty dancer, the songs revealed his growing talents as a gifted writer with his own idiosyncratic agenda. This was pop music, yes, but often with odd themes and structures that miraculously hooked you in. While some inevitably moaned that it wasn't *Thriller* part two, others eulogized its strengths, with some citing it as his best album. Michael had been storing ideas from the end of the Jacksons tour in 1984 onwards: 'Another Part Of Me' had featured in the *Captain EO* movie, and here replaced a track called 'Streetwalker' at the last minute, at the insistence of manager Frank DiLeo. Quincy Jones would use his experience to help the singer form his half-melodies and words into fully realized dynamic numbers. Only two came from outside sources: 'Just Good Friends' was penned by Graham Lyle and Terry Britten, and had Stevie Wonder guesting on vocals. The epic 'Man In The Mirror' was credited to Siedah Garrett and Glen Ballard, though

Below *Bad* had a tough act to follow, but Quincy helped Jackson manage it.

Right Michael unveiled a new, more aggressive image, involving leather and studs.

BAD

Michael's vocal performance in tandem with the mighty gospel arrangements is what makes it zing.

The rumours of duets with Prince and Barbra Streisand came to nothing, and when Quincy suggested Diana Ross, Michael declined as the pair were in the midst of a falling-out. Siedah Garrett's efforts on the duet 'I Just Can't Stop Loving You', the first single, are, however, a delight. Michael was "romantically linked" to her by the over-imaginative tabloids, as he was to the dancer he shimmied with in the video for 'The Way You Make Me Feel', Tatiana Thumbtzen, who went on to date Prince for real.

After 'I Just Can't Stop Loving You' had warmed audiences up with its brittle balladry, that 'Bad' video came in with an uppercut to popular culture's expectations. Michael's new publicist Bob Jones, ex-Motown, was an effective operator. He organized a TV special, *Michael Jackson: The Magic Returns*, and Scorsese was as cool and credible a name as was conceivable. The 'Bad' video took six weeks to complete, shooting at the Brooklyn Hoyt Schermerhorn subway station. In monochrome at first, Michael's character as a youth who's forsaken ghetto gangs for an education is taunted by his homeboys: "You don't down with us no more." Then the video bursts into colour, and Michael in his ensemble of leather, buckles and fingerless gloves sings and dances in the service of street peace and unity. The gang move on through Harlem, where it's said that Madonna, shooting the 'Who's That Girl?' video nearby, took time out to check out the scene. Trivia fans will note that among the extras in the mini-movie are Jeffrey "Moonwalk" Daniel and Wesley Snipes. Most were wowed by the video's electricity, though

Opposite Singing his heart out, as always.

Above Arriving on the six-week-long Bad video set.

“I ripped out a couple of solos, and he liked the first one. That was my choice too. He seemed to go on emotion rather than technique, which is how I’ve always worked.

RECORDED
January 5–July 9, 1987

RELEASED
August 31, 1987

LABEL
Epic

PERSONNEL
Michael Jackson (vocals, arrangements), Siedah Garrett, The Winans, and The Andraé Crouch Choir (backing vocals), Jerry Hey (horn arrangements), Christopher Currell, John Barnes, Graham Lyle, Terry Britten, Glen Ballard, and Jerry Hey (rhythm arrangements), plus various session musicians and backing singers

PRODUCERS
Quincy Jones, Michael Jackson

INITIAL CHART PERFORMANCES
US *Billboard* 200, No. 1; US *Billboard* R&B/Black Music, No.1; UK album charts No. 1

Quincy showed a lack of diplomacy in jokingly asking, "Is his underwear too tight?" The vocal high squeaks and beeps were as regular as a tic, and divided opinion.

'Dirty Diana' fuelled a storm of crazed gossip, some suggesting it was about Princess Diana, others wondering if it was aimed at his current feud (later resolved) with Ms Ross. As a rock-heavy close cousin to 'Beat It', it featured a shredding solo from Steve Stevens, best known as Billy Idol's axe hero. He himself wasn't sure why Eddie Van Halen hadn't got the gig again, but reported, "I ripped out a couple of solos, and he liked the first one. That was my choice too. He seemed to go on emotion rather than technique, which is how I've always worked." 'The Way You Make Me Feel' swaggeringly captured the sound of desire and lovestruck joy, while 'Speed Demon' was a funk-rock fever of fast driving. 'Liberian Girl' had in fact been readied a few years earlier, and considered for the Jacksons album *Victory*, and part of the melody hinted at an excerpt from 'Billie Jean'.

Above Michael worked by "emotion, not by technique".

Right With Siedah Garrett, who both sang and wrote key moments on this album.

Following pages: Left Bad to the bone: a contemporaneous jacket. **Right** With *Bad*'s success, Michael pointed the finger at any doubters.

BAD

'Smooth Criminal' was to become another Jackson signature song, after appearing as the theme song to his 1988 *Moonwalker* movie. It had been demoed under the name 'Al Capone', and again displays Michael's sometimes unfortunate lyrical interest in violence towards women. Despite the bloodstains and iffy content, the music is adrenalized, with Michael repeating, "Annie, are you OK?" like a man possessed. One suspects the song was another influenced by his keen film-watching. The video showcased a thirties-gangster scenario, choreographed by that man Jeffrey Daniel. Jackson liked the song and its dance routines so much that he played it on every tour from then on.

Not everybody "got" *Bad*: the *NME* spoke of "musical conservatism", adding, "Michael Jackson isn't God." *Rolling Stone* droned on about hype, its readers perversely voting it the year's worst album. Jackson never forgave the publication, even when they qualified their dislike by stressing it was the image that irked them, not the music. But generally, *Bad* was bathed in plaudits and awards, from the Brits to the American Music Awards. He was upset not to win the Album of the Year Grammy, especially after he'd sung 'The Way You Make Me Feel' and 'Man In The Mirror' live at the ceremony. "The night is yours," Quincy said, smiling, early in the evening. But it wasn't. When that coveted

> **From peace to paranoia, Bad is arguably the quintessential Jackson album. Every bit as much as Thriller, its presence bossed the eighties.**

award was presented to U2 by, of all people, Diana Ross, Michael was less than happy. As time has moved on, *Bad* is now established as one of Jackson's most titanic, influential and canonical works, an all-killer no-filler magic carpet ride. When Michael passed away in 2009, it was 'Man In The Mirror' that seemed ubiquitous, capturing something essential about the moment, and about the artist and the man.

From peace to paranoia, *Bad* is arguably the quintessential Jackson album. Every bit as much as *Thriller*, its presence bossed the eighties: 35 million sales worldwide, 10 million in the States – that's a phenomenon in its own right, by any standards. The last Jackson–Jones production saw the pop-transforming pairing go out with a Big Bad Bang.

Opposite Looking through the windows: a quiet moment on the set of the 'Bad' video.

Above Two giants of music history: with Stevie Wonder.

Following pages The Bad tour saw a more assertive, sexualised singer take the stage.

DANGEROUS (1991)

While the nineties were to be a turbulent decade for Michael, they began well with an album that has grown in acclaim as time has gone by. If in the moment it was difficult for critics and public alike to focus on the music and its messages, what with all the hullabaloo around Jackson's lifestyle and fame, *Dangerous* is now appreciated as an underrated work, and one which took pioneering steps for black music. As recently as 2018, the *Guardian* was hailing the album as one of his boldest artistic moves. The videos for 'Scream' and 'Remember The Time' were groundbreaking in themselves, while the first six tracks, collaborations with Teddy Riley, helped Jackson nail his post-Quincy sound in a fluid mix of new jack swing and what writer Joseph Vogel has called "grooves containing the punch of hip-hop, the swing of jazz and the chords of the black church." *Dangerous* sounded youthful, energized and streetwise.

Jackson and Jones had agreed to call time on their peerless phase together after *Bad*, and Jackson was hands-on in the new project, which took over a year to record. Teddy Riley and Bill Bottrell brought in-vogue, in-demand talents, while Jackson has composition credits on twelve of the fourteen tracks. At 77 minutes long, *Dangerous* also indicates the nineties custom of lengthy albums – effectively double albums – heralding the last-hurrah years of the Compact Disc format.

Michael was getting increasingly ambitious and candid with his themes, as racism, poverty and self-analysis were covered. The now-routine onslaught of singles and videos ensued, albeit with the ante upped on the latter, and *Dangerous* made its way onto the big leagues of sales by shifting over 30 million copies worldwide. As a mission to attract a younger urban audience, it was largely successful, though it arguably lost a portion of mainstream-leaning fans. Technically, while it contains obligatory detours into ballads and gospel, it's the biggest new jack swing album ever made.

Sony had now acquired CBS, and signed Jackson for reportedly the most lucrative contract the music business had yet known, with the singer securing an impressive royalty rate. The LA sessions took longer than any previous Jackson album, with Guns N' Roses guitarist Slash, who returned to guest on two tracks, describing a slow, laborious process, sample-heavy, with Michael only showing up "once a month". Riley – who Quincy Jones claims he'd recommended – even got Michael rapping. Yet, health problems diluted Jackson's enthusiasm at times. The album ended up a diverse but dynamic creature, with the new jack swing numbers contrasted by the rock of 'Black Or White' and 'Give In To Me', the big ballads 'Heal The World' and 'Gone Too Soon' and the smooth R&B slow jam of 'Remember The Time'.

The 'Black Or White' lead-single video prompted the first hot talking point, premiered to a global TV audience of 500 million viewers (it became his biggest hit since 'Billie Jean'). Michael inhabited the role of a kind of prophet or shaman, seen alongside Africans, Native Americans, Indians and even Russians proclaiming the wonders of diversity. Faces of varied races morph into other faces, as if to state skin colour is not what separates us. But when the video ends we see a black panther slinking down an alley, and then – startlingly – Michael grabs a crowbar and trashes a car, throws a garbage can through a store window (recalling a Spike Lee scene from *Do the Right Thing*) and tears his shirt open, all the while grunting, shrieking and touching himself suggestively, now almost feral. To lighten the mood, we then see Homer

Opposite Entering a turbulent nineties with optimism.

RECORDED
June 1989–October 1991

RELEASED
November 26, 1991

LABEL
Epic

PERSONNEL
Michael Jackson (vocals, arrangements), John Bahler Singers, Andraé Crouch Singers (backing vocals), Brad Buxer, George Del Barrio, Jerry Hey, Rhett Lawrence, Johnny Mandel, René Moore, David Paich, Marty Paich, Teddy Riley, Bruce Swedien (arrangements), plus various session musicians, singers and arrangers

PRODUCERS
Michael Jackson, Teddy Riley, Bill Bottrell, Bruce Swedien

INITIAL CHART PERFORMANCES
US *Billboard* 200, No. 1; US *Billboard* R&B/Black Music, No.1; UK album charts No. 1

Simpson take the remote from his son Bart and turn off the TV. Michael – and trusted director Jon Landis – were playing fast and loose here, risking the wrath of Michael's white family-friendly demographic. There was a rush of complaints, and Fox and MTV edited the video drastically. Said Jackson later, "I wanted to do a dance number where I could let out my frustration about injustice and prejudice and racism and bigotry. Within that dance, I became upset and let myself go." On another, less incendiary, more subtle level, the video for second single 'Remember The Time', directed by John Singleton and starring black luminaries Eddie Murphy, Magic Johnson and Iman, was also a pro-black statement. Set in ancient Egypt, it portrayed its black characters as royalty, upturning stereotypes. Singleton explained that "Michael wanted to do something to show us as we are – very beautiful people." Jordan appeared in the 'Jam' video, and Naomi Campbell shimmied suggestively with Michael in the enigmatically titled 'In The Closet'.

Dangerous feels like a coming-of-age album, which isn't to say it can claim to match his eighties high points, but it does sound like an artist of adult years, brimming with pride and immersing himself in the buzz of current black music – if you take the likes of sincere but overblown eco-hymn 'Heal The World' out of the equation, and the blast of Beethoven's *Ninth*, which heralds 'Will You Be There?', 'She Drives Me Wild' engaged rapping from Wreckx-n-Effect, which didn't feel out of place, and the title track oozed organic, uncontrived, sparing funk. *Rolling Stone* also heard this new maturity, referring to Michael as "a man, no longer a man-child, confronting his well-publicized demons and achieving transcendence through performance", while others noted its "abrasively unpredictable" rhythms. There were those who felt he sounded out of place on Riley's electronic-based burblers, but generally there was applause for the risks taken by *Dangerous*, which justified its name. More than is habitually credited, it tweaked the envelope of pop, shunting it into less cautious mannerisms.

Above Janet Jackson was also now a major star in her own right.

Right "A man, no longer a man-child", said *Rolling Stone*.

“I wanted to do a dance number where I could let out my frustration about injustice and prejudice and racism and bigotry.

Even the artwork, by Oregon pop-surrealist Mark Ryden, had the intensity and offbeat weirdness of, say, a seventies progressive-rock album, making you curious about what the album might contain even before you'd heard a note. *Dangerous* even overcame the surreal weirdness of over a quarter-million copies of stock being stolen at an LA airport just before its release date, to belatedly win Michael a "Grammy Legend" award in 1993, though he felt this didn't make up for the shortage of bona-fide Grammys. He had, as ever, hoped for a more definitively awed reaction, and compared his work here to that of Tchaikovsky on the *Nutcracker Suite*. He didn't make another full studio album for a decade, though this was as much down to personal stresses as any form of artist's block. He'd wanted *Dangerous* to be immortal, he said, to live for thousands of years, appreciated by children and parents of all races, across the planet. Perhaps at that time the rise of grunge bands such as Nirvana was the choice of youth, and the media's new hot topic, and its greatness went relatively overlooked. Yet now its chance-taking, refusal to play safe and all-round momentum sound more forcefully forward-thinking than almost any rock band, and its influence has pervaded. Jackson fans were right to keep the faith.

Previous pages: Left Michael appears on stage with executives from Pepsi and CBS records. **Right** Golden years: with Eddie Murphy and Iman for the "Remember The Time" video.

Above Trusty Liz Taylor remained a loyal friend through thick and thin.

Right Entertainment for all ages: Jackson attends a production of *Oliver!* in London.

HIStory: Past, Present and Future, Book 1 (1995)

Isolation, corporate avarice, media madness, environmentalism, suicide and social injustice: just some of the themes covered on the second disc of this peculiarly schizophrenic release, which tagged together a retrospective greatest hits set and a fascinating group of new songs made with top-of-the-range producers. *HIStory* – as its title is usually shortened to – became perceived primarily as a "Best of" compilation, whereas in its totality it was much more than that. Perhaps it would have been better understood as two separate albums. Nevertheless, it has sold over 20 million copies, and stands as the best-selling "double album" ever.

It therefore qualifies as a commercial juggernaut, despite emerging during troubled times for Michael's image – though by now it'll come as no surprise that Jackson himself thought sales were disappointing. The boom years of *Thriller* and *Bad* were not being matched by any up-and-comers in the business, so for a 37-year-old star to still be so popular was quite a statement. It also showed there was keen interest in not just his pop canon but his new work. Yes, people lapped up the likes of 'Billie Jean', 'The Way You Make Me Feel' and 'Don't Stop 'Til You Get Enough' all over again, but the contrasting outpourings from Michael's psyche that coloured the second album held a febrile, partly voyeuristic fascination.

Promotion from Sony was full-on. A video was released portraying the star marching at the front of an army of thousands of soldiers, as helicopters flew amid loud explosions and children screamed while girls swooned. As if that wasn't enough, huge statue-like effigies of Michael were floated along famous rivers in big cities: a forty-foot tall one sailed atop a boat down London's Thames, hogging headlines as hoped.

"I believe in perfection," he reiterated. "I try to create that in everything we do. I believe in perfect execution, and when we don't get at least 99.9%, I get really upset." He showcased his musicianship more on this new material. For the first time on an album, he played guitars, keyboards and synthesisers, and percussion. Again there was the dichotomy between his biting and sugary sides, from the tenacious 'Tabloid Junkie' to the cheesy if tender Charlie Chaplin ballad 'Smile' (which Jermaine was to sing at Michael's funeral in 2009). Yet, the fact that you couldn't settle, that you could never predict where Michael would go next, added to the energies at play.

'Scream', the first single, was a striking shriek of intent. A duet with sister, Janet, by now a major star herself, was a truly fierce release. The video – at $5 million, the costliest in pop to date – was a whirlpool of stark aggression and loaded charisma. In shiny black and white, its fusion of science fiction and impassioned performance saw both Jacksons being overt in their sexually charged posturing, and take-no-prisoners taunts. They both gleamed with star quality, and it remains one of the most unforgettable videos of their careers. (It won three MTV awards and a Grammy). The song spelled out Michael's rage at press intrusion and the dubious stories with which the tabloids tormented him. Its refrain of "Stop pressuring me" sounds like a man who simply has to vent or else he'll implode.

Yet, again, he balances this pugilistic side of his nature with an inspirational ballad that some adore but others consider schmaltzy. 'You Are Not Alone' was the second single, and became the first-ever to debut at number one on the *Billboard* chart. Its profile was boosted by Michael's marriage to Lisa-Marie Presley, a union they exhibited in the song's video. Therein, the pair appeared almost naked, canoodling as if to defy doubters and loudly display a genuine physical attraction to each other. There was a third enormous single in the form of 'Earth Song', which flagged up another overriding theme of Michael's: let's save the planet. It sold a million, and gained Britain's coveted Christmas number-one spot, back then a big deal. Its message crossed territories, translated easily. Its over-the-top video gave Michael a chance to enact his best, wind-machine-assisted Messiah poses as he championed the environment, and begged us to think what kind of Earth we'd be leaving our children, and their children.

Less all-pleasing was 'They Don't Care About Us', an angry anthem whose lyrics – surely accidentally – ran into trouble, drawing accusations of anti-Semitism for the way the word "Jew" was used. Michael explained in an articulate not-quite apology: "The idea that these lyrics could be deemed objectionable is extremely hurtful to me, and misleading. The song is in fact about the pain of prejudice and hate, and is a way to draw attention to social and political problems. I am the voice of the accused and the attacked. I am the voice of everyone. I am the skinhead, I am the Jew, I am the black man, I am the white man. I am not the one

---

Previous pages If anyone merited a greatest hits package, it was the King of Pop.

Right In the spotlight: pondering his career retrospective.

who was attacking. It is about the injustices to young people and how the system can wrongfully accuse them. I am angry and outraged that I could be so misinterpreted." Later, he told a reporter, "It's not anti-Semitic because I'm not a racist person. I could never be a racist; I love all races." The controversy ran on, until Michael issued an actual apology – "I apologize to anyone who might have been hurt" – and then furthermore returned to the studio and re-recorded, for future copies of the record, the offending excerpt of "Jew me" as "do me", and "Kike me" as "Strike me". Spike Lee's video for the track boldly highlighted human-rights abuses.

'Stranger In Moscow' couldn't possibly be as controversial, despite its line "Stalin's tomb won't let me be", and turned a poem Michael had written into another veiled retaliation at the press. Writing on tour in Moscow, he'd used Russian imagery and symbolism to express within the slow, synth-based song his sense of fearfulness and alienation. He was, reckoned critics, "angry, miserable, tortured, inflammatory, furious about what he calls [in the song] 'a swift and sudden fall from grace'." Some reviews of the track spoke of its "real genius", and even Rod Temperton, who knew a trick or two about songwriting, called it Michael's best song. Nick Brandt's rainswept video, shot in LA, emphasized the star's sense of isolation. "Even at home I'm lonely," he said in J. Randy Taraborrelli's biography. "I sit in my room sometimes and cry. It's so hard to make friends. I sometimes walk around the neighbourhood at night, just hoping to find someone to talk to. But I just end up coming home."

Little wonder, then, that he found some solace in Chaplin's 'Smile', and in recording The Beatles' 'Come Together'. He was still making his own history: the ensuing *HIStory* tour, across 58 countries but not the 'States, played to five million ecstatic fans, who were closer to hysteria. The album was a paradox of sorts – the joyful classic danceable hits on one disc, these mostly punchy, twitchy new songs on the other – but if the press were on his back, the public were very much on his side.

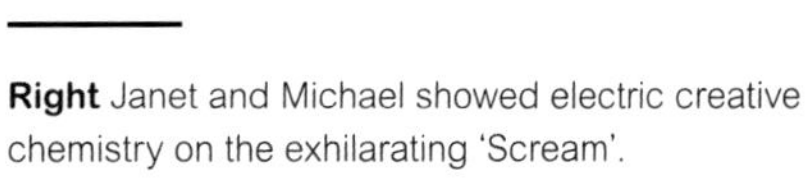

Right Janet and Michael showed electric creative chemistry on the exhilarating 'Scream'.

Following pages Into the future: this set combined old hits with new directions.

RECORDED
Disc One, 1978–1991, Disc Two, 1988–1995

RELEASED
June 16, 1995

LABEL
Epic/MJJ Productions

PERSONNEL
Michael Jackson (vocals, guitar, arrangements), Dallas Austin, John Bahler, Glen Ballard, John Barnes, Elmer Bernstein, Brad Buxer, David Foster, David Paich, Marty Paich, Quincey Jones, Jerry Hey, Teddy Riley (arrangements), John Bahler, Boyz II Men, Chauna Bryant, Roger Bumpass, Caleena Campbell, Reeve Carney, Andraé Crouch, The Winans (backing vocals), The Notorious B.I.G. (guest artist) plus various session musicians, singers and arrangers

PRODUCERS
Michael Jackson, Janet Jackson, Jimmy Jam and Terry Lewis, Dallas Austin, Bruce Swedien, Rene Moore, David Foster, Bill Bottrell

INITIAL CHART PERFORMANCES
US *Billboard* 100, No. 1; US *Billboard* R&B, No. 1; UK albums, No. 1

BLOOD ON THE DANCE FLOOR: HIStory IN THE MIX (1997)

There's some debate as to whether this intriguing oddity counts as a full album, as it consists of five then-new songs plus eight remixes of tracks from the two-year-old *HIStory…* collection. By Jackson standards, it didn't receive much promotion, and there was a general shrug from the media, who thought of it as a placeholder, a stopgap. Again, the decision to split between new and reheated material confused rather than wowed, but with six million sales it stands as the best-selling remix album ever – even if its quintet of originals should technically discount it from that status.

The irony is that those new songs are darkly compelling, and there's half of what could have been an attractive album here. Lyrically, Michael addressed sex, drugs, painkillers and paranoia to the point where some overexcited critics drew reference to Marilyn Manson and Nine Inch Nails. Others accused him of playing the victim in a world he perceived as full of manipulative women and conspiratorial forces. Somewhere within the album was a cry for help from an artist struggling to cope, and it might have made for truly great art – and a healthier release valve for Michael – if he'd been allowed to express these frustrations more fully, without the compromise of focus-grouped ballads and remixes.

So despite the loyalty of fans, *Blood On The Dance Floor* was perceived as a marketing concept, rather than a concept album. Just as *HIStory…* would have made more impact as two separate albums, this was diluted by its caution in tempering the daring new material with the more overtly commercial remixes. In being only "half new", it reduced the sense of event that had always announced Michael's releases. The title track itself was in fact his best single in some time. It kicked, whipped and crackled, rediscovering the narcissistic sass that had informed his pomp. Teddy Riley produced, and succeeded in cooking up a kind of wicked step-sister to 'Billie Jean'. A girl called Susie is going around stabbing "hot men" dancers with a switchblade, and one can only hope Michael's inspiration was just the spooky movies he seemed now so keen on. The song's highly sexualized video, with Michael dancing with an overtly seductive Sybil Azur, drew some half-hearted controversy, but nothing to frighten the horses. Certainly, those creepy horror themes returned on 'Ghosts' and 'Is It Scary', both of which were staccato and compulsive. As a singer he threw himself committedly into his whoops, breaths, gasps and groin-clutches. There are phases where he's completely in his element, as powerful as his peaks on his Quincy-era work. 'Superfly Sister' doesn't quite take off as it wants to, but 'Morphine' (now there's a title to wonder about) rocks, convincingly, with Slash returning on guitar, before gliding into an almost classical feel then hammering back like thunder. Echoing 'State Of Shock', it's an underrated moment in his canon.

The remixes of the likes of 'Scream', 'Stranger In Moscow' and 'Earth Song' are negligible when delivered by names like Tee, Tony Moran and Hani. Wyclef Jean of Fugees was ubiquitous at the time; his reboot of 'Bad', despite dropping in a line from 'Beat It', isn't good. Best effort comes from Jimmy Jam and Terry Lewis who make 'Scream' even louder, with a sample from Sly and The Family Stone. The net project irritates, though, by dropping in the fashionable words "club" and "house" more frequently than a golf club veteran.

Jackson had been on the epic *HIStory* world tour, which may be one reason for the album feeling somewhat unfinished, the tracks mixed on the hoof in various countries. Yet, its better bursts remind us of everything that was imaginative about the

Opposite The new songs were the new album's highlights.

RECORDED
1991–1997

RELEASED
May 20, 1997

LABEL
Epic/MJJ Productions

PERSONNEL
Michael (vocals, arrangements), Slash, Wyclef Jean (guitars) plus various session musicians, and additional mixing producers

PRODUCERS
Michael Jackson, Teddy Riley, Jimmy Jam and Terry Lewis, Bruce Swedien, Rene Moore, Dallas Austin, David Foster, Bill Bottrell, R. Kelly

INITIAL CHART PERFORMANCES
US *Billboard* 200, No. 24; US *Billboard* R&B/Hip-Hop, No. 12; UK albums, No. 1

star. The lyrics of 'Morphine' discussing the use of Demerol – "trust in me, just in me… close your eyes and drift away". The 'Thriller'-rekindling short film for 'Ghosts', which was co-written by Jackson and Stephen King, debuted in London. (The promotional campaign did go light on America, believing other countries to now be more sympathetic to Michael). And best of all, that title track, originally mooted for the *Dangerous* album, which again fared better outside the US; a single that set a scarlet-suited Michael on a new jack swing stage and allowed his talents to flourish.

While the album was a number one in six countries, including Britain, its low profile in the 'States saw it fail to make the Top 20. That single, similarly, gave him his seventh UK number one, while struggling in the US, where perhaps people were now more obsessed with Michael's private life than his red-hot recordings. Yet, despite this, it's a groove that gets anyone's blood pumping.

Above and right Good on the dance floor: Michael echoes the Moonwalk days.

INVINCIBLE (2001)

You can't touch me, 'cos I'm untouchable," sang Michael opening the last album of new material of his lifetime. "You'll never break me cos I'm unbreakable." He was, as so often in his adult years, under intense pressure, but came out to face the new century defiant and fighting, as the album's bravado title attested. A decade after *Dangerous*, it took a lot of time and work to make, the project having been started in 1997, but went to number one in eleven territories, including the US and the UK, and was double platinum within three months. Its recorded sales are now around seven to eight million. And, yet, by Jackson's standards, this was considered a failure. Perhaps the *Sydney Morning Herald* got close to the truth when it protested that nearly every other artist would think "all their Christmases had come at once" with such sales figures. However, "Michael Jackson... is branded a failure in the industry and media. Unfair? Yes, of course... his *Invincible* figures are better than those of 95% of the thousands of artists released each year and would provide a healthy retirement fund for anyone. That 'failure' tag is consistently applied with comparisons with *Thriller* (100 million copies) and *Bad*..."

Invincible cost a reported $30 million to produce, making it debatably the most expensive album yet made. Jackson getting into a heated series of disagreements with Sony didn't help, when it came to their promoting the end result. The latest set of problems began when the singer learned that the rights to the masters of his back catalogue with the label, which he'd understood would soon revert to his ownership, didn't in fact do so for several more years. He contacted the lawyer who'd worked with him on the initial 1991 deal, only to find that lawyer was working with Sony, in what might be described as a conflict of interest. So Jackson, furious, decided to leave the Sony group as soon as the album was released. They retaliated by minimising promotion and even nixing some planned single releases. They argued that they'd spent a fortune on a "disappointing" project. Jackson ranted back that Sony boss Tommy Mottola was a "racist" and a "devil", and that the company would have backed the record more if he was a white artist. His brothers supported him on this, but many even within his own circle were shocked at his comments and thought they were born of anger rather than reason. "Ludicrous, spiteful and hurtful," said Sony. Little wonder then that artist and label parted on bad terms. Mottola was no longer head of Sony one year later, but opinions differ as to whether this was related to his fall-out with Jackson.

Sony argued that they did in fact promote *Invincible* with gusto, and their releasing it in five different coloured sleeves went towards supporting that view. Three singles, 'You Rock My World', 'Cry' and 'Butterflies' emerged, though with limited releases. The first was by far the most successful – and the best – although in the States it achieved a Top Ten position based on airplay alone, not being given a commercial release. There was a slinky disco-pop groove to it; while some critics were keen to jump on the fashionable Jackson-bashing bandwagon, others correctly called it "finely sculpted" and "exquisite". The trouble was that people were struggling to hear the music on its own terms, distracted as they were by the constant media hullaballoo around Michael's persona and private life.

Invincible had been perceived as a "comeback", being a fully new album. It was dedicated to a teenage victim of racism, a friend of a friend of Jackson. "May we continue to remember not to judge man by the colour of his skin, but the content of his character", ran the pointed dedication. On the tracks within, Michael worked with many of the new millennium's most talented and in-vogue producers. They were bubbling and burbling with restless rhythm tracks. He'd frequently recorded from October 1997 onwards, one of the most productive sessions taking place with Rodney Jerkins at the Hit Factory in Miami. Jerkins said Jackson had wanted to take fresh directions, to go "edgier". Among the other hot, name producers were Babyface, R. Kelly and Teddy Riley (again). The robust results were an intoxicating, often compelling brew of R&B and urban dance. Hip-hop made an entrance, as did rap, but elsewhere there were old-school nods to "adult contemporary". At 77 minutes, *Invincible* crams in a whole lot of ideas, swinging between dynamic, modern-feeling music and syrupy ballads. "With all that I've been through, I'm still around," states Michael early on, placing a flag in the ground of this new turf.

Contrasts collide and clash. 'Privacy' is a clearly autobiographical, pumped-up venting about tabloid lies and media intrusion, while 'The Lost Children' is another of Michael's songs about children needing protection. 'Whatever Happens' gives us a jittery, anxious protagonist. 'You Are My Life' is addressed adoringly to his children Prince and Paris. With 'Cry' and 'Butterflies' rather maudlin ballads, "You Rock My World" ran the show in terms of inviting people into

Right Blue sky thinking: *Invincible* was arguably an underrated comeback album.

the album and recommending it as a fun experience. Rodney Jerkins and Fred Jerkins III were among the co-writers of the track, but production credits were shared between Darkchild and Michael. Its video did not carry any signs of Sony scrimping, as its thirteen minutes gave us Chris Tucker goofing around with Michael, and even a glimpse of the usually reclusive Marlon Brando, whose odd friendship with Michael was in its salad days.

As always, reactions were divided, with some acknowledging its spark and rejuvenated feel; others bemoaning the excess of long-winded ballads. Those

RECORDED
November 1997–August 2001 (multiple sessions)

RELEASED
October 30, 2001

LABEL
Epic

PERSONNEL
Michael Jackson (vocals, various instruments, arrangements), David Campbell (arrangements), Marsha Ambrosius, Maxi Anderson, Gloria Augustus, Tom Bahler, Babyface, Edie Lehmann Boddicker, Robert Bolyard, Brandy, LaShawn Daniels, Valerie Doby, Yvonne Williams, Mario Vasquez, Howard McCrary, Linda McCrary, Sam McCrary, Dr Freeze (backing vocals), Slash (guitar) plus various session musicians, singers and arrangers

PRODUCERS
Michael Jackson, Rodney Jerkins, Teddy Riley, Dr. Freeze, Andreao "Fanatic" Heard, Nate Smith, Andre Harris, Kenneth "Babyface" Edmonds, R. Kelly, Richard Stites

INITIAL CHART PERFORMANCES
US *Billboard*, No. 1; US *Billboard* R&B, No. 1; UK charts, No. 1

in the middle placed it as a near-miss, or balanced the sentimental songs against the superior, more interesting rhythmic rumpuses. There was just one Grammy nomination (for the vocal performance on 'You Rock My World', which lost to James Taylor). It was the eleventh best-selling album of 2001. People were kinder, and fiercely so, with hindsight: a few months after Michael's death, *Billboard*'s readers voted it Album of the Decade. The last album by Michael in motion, when distanced from the hype and tabloid trauma of its time, now sounds intelligent, idiosyncratic and often invigorated. While the ballads weigh it down, there's a real attempt in the spicier material to fly. *Invincible* won the long game.

Right You rock my world: fans felt the heat even if critics didn't.

THIS IS IT (2009)

This Is It should have been a joyous celebration of The King of Pop's comeback. As it transpired, the release of the soundtrack to the film of Michael's rehearsals for the intended 02 Arena concerts served as a eulogy. Just four months after his death, the two-disc set debuted at number one in fourteen countries, becoming the third best-selling album of the year worldwide, the title track winning a Grammy nomination.

It was one of six previously unreleased tracks, with the bulk of the release being made up of previous hits and popular numbers in a kind of wishful-thinking set list. What a set it would have been. The title song, co-written with veteran Paul Anka back in 1983, appeared in vocal and orchestral versions, while the second disc's four "new" songs were three demos plus the poem 'Planet Earth', which had appeared in print on the sleeve artwork of *Dangerous*.

Reception bounced between a positive response to the demos' interesting arrangements, to criticism aimed at a crass cash-in. *This Is It* had its moments, but it obviously wasn't the "It" fans had been hoping for earlier in the year.

RECORDED
1978–2009

RELEASED
October 26, 2009

LABEL
Epic/Sony/MJJ

PERSONNEL
Michael Jackson, Quincy Jones, Teddy Riley, Rod Temperton, Siedah Garrett, Jerry Hey, The Jacksons plus various session musicians

PRODUCERS
Michael Jackson, John McClain

INITIAL CHART PERFORMANCES
US *Billboard*, No. 1; US *Billboard* R&B/Hip-Hop, No. 1; UK charts, No. 3

MICHAEL (2010)

The first full posthumous album of "new" or "previously unreleased" material met with a wall of doubts and scepticism. Michael's own family questioned its validity, with Randy Jackson questioning whether it was even his brother's voice on some tracks. "I immediately said it wasn't his voice," he stated. The authenticity or otherwise of what are known as the "Cascio tracks" – 'Breaking News', 'Keep Your Head Up' and 'Monster' – has prompted much controversy, with the rest of the Jackson family and the musican will.i.am backing Randy. Allegedly recorded in the Cascio family's basement, the tracks were defended by Sony and by Teddy Riley, who suggested a processing technique used on the vocals was causing the issue. By 2013, Riley, too, was apologising, claiming he'd been "set up". Joe Jackson and will.i.am went on to criticize the album, with the latter calling it "disrespectful", as Michael wouldn't have given his blessing to unfinished material. Foo Fighters' Dave Grohl even joined in, calling it "not cool" that he was credited as playing drums on '(I Can't Make It) Another Day' when the released version didn't feature his contribution.

RECORDED
1982–2009 (posthumous re-workings in 2010)

RELEASED
January 24, 2010

LABEL
Epic/Sony/MJJ

PERSONNEL
Michael Jackson (vocals, arrangements), David Campbell , Benjamin Wright (arrangements), Dave Grohl (drums), Curtis "50 Cent" Jackson, Lenny Kravitz (vocals) plus various session musicians and singers

PRODUCERS
Akon, Brad Buxer, Eddie Cascio, Neff-U, John McClain, Lenny Kravitz, Teddy Riley, C. "Tricky" Stewart, Giorgio Tuinfort, Michael Jackson

INITIAL CHART PERFORMANCES
US *Billboard*, No. 3; US *Billboard* R&B/Hip-Hop, No. 1; UK charts, No. 4

So what are the positives on the perhaps misguided *Michael*? Well, the production from the likes of Akon, Lenny Kravitz and, of course, Riley keeps the music modern and clean, proving that Jackson had been keen to retain a contemporary edge. Most material came from the *Invincible* era. The singles released – 'Hold My Hand', 'Hollywood Tonight' and 'Behind The Mask' – were solid if not spectacular. The artwork by Kadir Nelson paid homage to Jackson's position as "a symbol of royalty, his musical history unfolding behind him". Reviews ranged from "a great deal better than anybody had any right to expect" to "emaciated, effects-laden" and "if this decent-enough album is the best of the bunch, things are going to get ugly from here on in".

Ultimately, diehard fans were going to clutch it to their hearts, regardless. The opener, 'Hold My Hand', began with "This life don't last forever", and the final track 'Much Too Soon' ended with, "I guess I learned my lesson much too soon." Poignant moments like that that spoke to believers. The album's sales were at first promising, but it fell away quickly.

XSCAPE (2014)

Xscape was an altogether more considered and classy affair than *Michael*. Time was taken to consider its merits as an overall package, and it felt like a set of songs that deserved to be heard. Jackson's voice was respectfully placed centre stage, while the productions seemed less contrived and more natural. It wasn't uniformly great, but a track, 'Do You Know Where Your Children Are' – which had narrowly failed to make the cut for both the *Bad* and *Dangerous* albums – worked both as a juicy jam and as a compelling, even provocative lyric. And the launch single, Love Never Felt So Good', was a breezy dancefloor strut that recalled his classic disco-soul era, with charm to burn. It was another co-composition with Paul Anka from 1983, which Johnny Mathis had released in 1984. Now Michael's old demo was given a disco-style backing track, with DJ-rapper Timbaland contributing. The song made Michael the first artist ever to have a Top 10 *Billboard* hit in five different decades. (Six if you include The Jackson 5). A duet of the same song was released, with Justin Timberlake.

Elsewhere, the album showed the guiding hand of executive producer L.A. Reid, with Rodney Jerkins and Stargate involved in production. 'Loving You' was recorded just prior to the *Bad* album. 'A Place With No Name', from 1998, wilfully echoes America's soft-rock hit 'A Horse With No Name'. 'Blue Gangsta' was an off-cut from *Invincible*, as was the title track. Jerkins slips in samples of 'You Rock My World'. 'Slave To The Rhythm', a title always highly suited to Michael, was no relation to the Grace Jones gem. As critics noted, the album in the main sensitively showcased Jackson's ageless vocals without smothering them in an excess of electronic trickery. It went gold in the UK, and has sold half a million in America.

RECORDED
1983–2001 (posthumous re-workings 2013–14)

RELEASED
May 9, 2014

LABEL
Epic/Sony/MJJ

PERSONNEL
Michael Jackson (vocals, keyboards, drums), LaShawn Daniels (backing vocals), Frank van der Haijden (orchestral arrangements) plus various session musicians

PRODUCERS
Michael Jackson, Paul Anka, Kenneth Edmonds, Dr. Freeze, Jerone "J-Roc" Harmon, Rodney Jerkins, Daniel Jones, King Solomon Logan, Cory Rooney, Giorgio Tuinfort, Timbaland, Stargate

INITIAL CHART PERFORMANCES
US *Billboard*, No. 2; US *Billboard* R&B/Hip-Hop, No. 1; UK charts, No. 1

aseball!

Left Michael's talent displayed itself early, and the young boy lit up stages and TV screens with his astonishing voice and James Brown-inspired moves. Yet this was one child star who'd stick around. This shiny outfit and cap were the very height of fashion during the Motown days.

Above By the time of this portrait, taken in 1978, Michael was sporting a proud Afro hairstyle and bringing on the suave. "My goal in life," he said at the time, "is to give the world what I was lucky enough to receive – the ecstasy of divine union through music and dance."

Following pages A nimble Michael moves for the camera in 1979, the year in which *Off The Wall* announced him as a truly major player. He's certainly starting to look the part. Even without the imminent tuxedo and black tie, he's echoing the newly mature elegance and sophistication of his music.

Left It's *Thriller* time. Not yet transformed by John Landis into a werewolf, Michael sports a seemingly casual, preppy jacket. Yet our knowledge of the mutations his image now went through at a rapid pace grants it an iconic status. As if any of us need that big M to remind us of his name.

Right The red leather jacket worn in the 'Beat It' video, wherein Michael played peacemaker between two rival gangs in a modern twist on the famous *West Side Story* scenario. He was especially fond of this jacket, wearing it again at the *Dreamgirls* premiere in LA in 1983, where he was photographed with both Cher and Liberace.

AMOU

Above The cover image for *Bad*, the much-anticipated follow-up album to *Thriller*, revealed a tougher, grittier Jackson. A riot of leather, belts, buckles and studded gloves showed his new affinity with rock music and his refusal to stay within conventional genre boundaries.

Right The subsequent Bad tour broke box-office records. As if the laser shows and pyrotechnic explosions weren't enough, Michael, hoisted by wires, appeared to be flying. The eternal Peter Pan didn't skimp on the heavyweight-champion belt and trouser studs.

> "The Dangerous world tour was marketed as 'the most spectacular, state-of-the-art show the world has ever seen'. It was again sponsored by Pepsi, who paid Michael in the region of $20 million.

Right The *Dangerous* tour, running almost eighteen months, showcased a look that may have encouraged the "Wacko Jacko" detractors but also undeniably made a bold statement. We all want our pop stars to be larger than life: in this military-inspired jacket, single glove and gold codpiece, Michael was anything but the boy next door.

"I wanted to do an album that was like Tchaikovsky's Nutcracker Suite, so that a thousand years from now people would still be listening to it. Something that would live forever.

Left Just as Michael's music mixed pop, rock, street grooves and Tin Pan Alley sentiment, so his appearance began to jumble together styles in an intriguing and radical fashion. The military, psychedelic *Sgt. Pepper* vibe was still a factor, but there's both androgyny and pensiveness about his aura now.

Left That unforgettable, magical "Moonwalk" moment was of course, for many, the night Michael went from superstar to megastar. The Jacksons could contain him no longer, as he raised the bar on the razzle-dazzle of dance moves. He made his hat work miracles, and even his hero Fred Astaire praised his performance.

Right The *HIStory* tour, which began in September 1996, was no less spectacular than its predecessors. On stage, Michael would emerge from a pod-like spacecraft clad as a gold astronaut, removing his helmet to the sound of deafening roars and screams from excited fans. His love of science-fiction movies clearly fed his creative imagination.

Right At the 1995 MTV Video Awards, Michael had worn a spangly jacket for a teasing section of 'Billie Jean' but then made a quick change for 'Dangerous'. Leading his troupe of similarly besuited backing dancers here, he commits fully to his trademark crotch-grabbing action. The white socks have endured from earlier, more innocent days.

Left An intimate portrait of a leather jacket-clad Michael seems to reveal a blend of thoughtful melancholy and effortless grace. It makes sense that in Summer 2018, London's National Portrait Gallery opened an exhibition of art inspired by the star, including work by Andy Warhol and David LaChapelle.

Left Michael was always insistent on thanking his loyal fans for their support. Dressed here in a distinguished, mature suit, by his standards understated, he seems to be cupping his hands in a gesture of gratitude.

Above Michael Jackson was one of the most significant figures in the history of popular culture. Here, he's seen scarlet-shirted in 2002, performing at a Democratic National Committee fundraiser. August 29, 2018 would have been his 60th birthday.

APPE

NDIX

ALBUMS

WITH THE JACKSON 5

Diana Ross Presents The Jackson 5
December 18, 1969
Motown

Side A:
Zip-A-Dee-Doo-Dah
Nobody
I Want You Back
Can You Remember
Standing in the Shadows Of Love
You've Changed

Side B:
My Cherie Amour
Who's Lovin' You
Chained
(I Know) I'm Losing You
Stand!
Born To Love You

Bonus track on reissue:
Oh, I've Been Bless'd

ABC
May 8, 1970
Motown

The Love You Save
One More Chance
ABC
2-4-6-8
(Come 'Round Here) I'm The One You Need
Don't Know Why I Love You
Never Had A Dream Come True
True Love Can Be Beautiful
La-La (Means I Love You)
I'll Bet You
I Found That Girl
The Young Folks

Bonus track on reissue:
Oh, I've Been Bless'd

Third Album
September 8, 1970
Motown

Side one:
I'll Be There
Ready Or Not (Here I Come)
Oh How Happy
Bridge Over Troubled Water
Can I See You In The Morning

Side two:
Goin' Back To Indiana
How Funky Is Your Chicken
Mama's Pearl
Reach In
The Love I saw In You Was Just A Mirage
Darling Dear

Bonus tracks on reissue:
Sugar Daddy
I'm So Happy

Jackson 5 Christmas Album
October 15, 1970
Motown

Have Yourself A Merry Little Christmas
Santa Claus Is Comin' To Town
The Christmas Song
Up On The House Top
Frosty The Snowman
The Little Drummer Boy
Rudolph The Red-Nosed Reindeer
Christmas Won't Be The Same This Year
Give Love On Christmas Day
Someday At Christmas
I Saw Mommy Kissing Santa Claus

Bonus tracks on reissue:
Season's Greetings From Michael Jackson (2009)
Little Christmas Tree (2003)
Season's Greetings From Tito Jackson (2009)
Up On The House Top (Re-edit) (2009)
Season's Greetings From Jackie Jackson (2009)
Rudolph The Red-Nosed Reindeer (stripped mix) (2009)
Season's Greetings From Jermaine Jackson (2009)
Someday At Christmas (Stripped Mix) (2009)
Give Love On Christmas Day (A Cappella) (2009)
J5 Christmas Medley (2009)

Maybe Tomorrow
April 12, 1971
Motown

Maybe Tomorrow
She's Good
Never Can Say Goodbye
The Wall
Petals
Sixteen Candles
(We've Got) Blue Skies
My Little Baby
It's Great To Be Here
Honey Chile
I Will Find A Way

Bonus tracks on reissue:
Sugar Daddy
I'm So Happy

Goin' Back To Indiana (Live)
September 29, 1971
Motown

I Want You Back
Maybe Tomorrow
The Day Basketball Was Saved
Stand!
I Want To Take You Higher
Feelin' Alright
Medley: Walk On / The Love You Save
Goin' Back To Indiana

Bonus tracks on reissue:
Love Song
Who's Lovin' You

Lookin' Through The Windows
May 17, 1972
Motown

Side one:
Ain't Nothing Like The Real Thing
Lookin' Through The Windows
Don't Let Your Baby Catch You
To Know
Doctor My Eyes

Side two:
Little Bitty Pretty One
E-Ne-Me-Ne-Mi-Ne-Moe
If I Have To Move A Mountain
Don't Want To See Tomorrow
Children of the Light
I Can Only Give You Love

Opposite Michael strikes an appropriately winning pose during the Victory tour in 1984.

Bonus tracks on reissue:
Love Song
Who's Lovin' You

Skywriter
March 29, 1973
Motown

Side one:
Skywriter
Hallelujah Day
The Boogie Man
Touch
Corner Of The Sky

Side two:
I Can't Quit Your Love
Uppermost
World Of Sunshine
Ooh, I'd Love To Be With You
You Made Me What I Am

Bonus tracks on reissue:
Pride And Joy
Love's Gone Bad
Love Is The Thing You Need

The Jackson 5 in Japan (Live) / Michael Jackson with the Jackson 5 Live
October 31, 1973 (Japan)
1986 (UK)

Side A:
Introduction/We're Gonna Have A Good Time
Lookin' Through The Windows
Got To Be There
Medley: I Want You Back/ ABC/The Love You Save
Daddy's Home
Superstition

Side B:
Ben
Papa Was A Rollin' Stone
That's How Love Goes
Never Can Say Goodbye
Ain't That Peculiar
I Wanna Be Where You Are

G.I.T.: Get It Together
September 21, 1973
Motown

Side one:
Get It Together
Don't Say Goodbye Again
Reflections
Hum Along And Dance

Side two:
Mama I Got A Brand New Thing (Don't Say No)
It's Too Late To Change The Time
You Need Love Like I Do (Don't You)
Dancing Machine

Dancing Machine
September 5, 1974
Motown

Side one:
I Am Love
Whatever You Got, I Want
She's A Rhythm Child
Dancing Machine

Side two:
The Life Of The Party
What You Don't Know
If I Don't Love You This Way
It All Begins and Ends With Love
The Mirrors Of My Mind

Bonus tracks on reissue:
Through Thick And Thin
Forever Came Today (Disc-o-Tech #3 Remix)

Moving Violation
May 15, 1975
Motown

Side one:
Forever Came Today
Moving Violation
(You Were Made) Especially For Me
Honey Love

Side two:
Body Language
All I Do Is Think Of You
Breezy
Call Of The Wild
Time Explosion

Bonus tracks on reissue:
Through Thick And Thin
Forever Came Today (Disc-o-Tech #3 Remix)

Boogie (Compilation)
January 16, 1979
Motown / Natural Resources

Side A:
Love's Gone Bad
I Ain't Gonna Eat Out My Heart Anymore
ABC
I Was Made To Love Her
One Day I'll Marry You

Side B:
Never Can Say Goodbye
Oh, I've Been Bless'd
Penny Arcade
Just Because I Love You
Dancing Machine

WITH THE JACKSONS

The Jacksons
November 5, 1976
Epic / Philadelphia International Records

Side one:
Enjoy Yourself
Think Happy
Good Times
Keep On Dancing
Blues Away

Side two:
Show You The Way to Go
Living Together
Strength Of One Man
Dreamer
Style Of Life

Goin' Places
October 8, 1977
Epic / Philadelphia International Records

Side one:
Music's Takin' Over
Goin' Places
Different Kind Of Lady
Even Though You're Gone

Side two:
Jump For Joy
Heaven Knows I Love You, Girl
Man Of War
Do What You Wanna
Find Me a Girl

Destiny
December 17, 1978
Epic

Blame It on the Boogie
Push Me Away
Things I Do For You
Shake Your Body (Down To The Ground)
Destiny
Bless His Soul
All Night Dancin'
That's What You Get (For Being Polite)

Bonus tracks on reissue:
Blame It On The Boogie (John Luongo Disco Mix)
Shake Your Body (Down To The Ground) (John Luongo Disco Mix)

Triumph
September 26, 1980
Epic

Can You Feel It
Lovely One
Your Ways
Everybody
This Place Hotel
Time Waits For No One
Walk Right Now
Give It Up
Wondering Who

Bonus tracks on reissue:
This Place Hotel (Single Version)
Walk Right Now (John Luongo Disco Mix)
Walk Right Now (John Luongo Instrumental Mix)

The Jacksons Live!
November 11, 1981
Epic

Opening/Can You Feel It
Things I Do for You
Off The Wall
Ben
This Place Hotel
She's Out Of My Life
Movie And Rap, including excerpts of: I Want You Back/Never Can Say Goodbye/Got to Be There
Medley: I Want You Back/ ABC/The Love You Save
I'll Be There
Rock With You
Lovely One
Workin' Day And Night
Don't Stop 'Til You Get Enough
Shake Your Body (Down To The Ground)

Victory
July 2, 1984
Epic

Torture
Wait
One More Chance
Be Not Always
State Of Shock
We Can Change The World
The Hurt
Body

2300 Jackson Street
May 28, 1989
Epic

Michael only featured on the title song for this album, 2300 Jackson Street.

SOLO

Got to Be There
January 24, 1972
Motown

Ain't No Sunshine
I Wanna Be Where You Are
Girl Don't Take Your Love From Me
In Our Small Way
Got To Be There
Rockin' Robin
Wings Of My Love
Maria (You Were The Only One)
Love Is Here And Now You're Gone
You've Got A Friend

Ben
August 4, 1972
Motown

Ben
Greatest Show On Earth
People Make The World Go 'Round'
We've Got A Good Thing Going
Everybody's Somebody's Fool
My Girl
What Goes Around Comes Around
In Our Small Way
Shoo-Be-Doo-Be-Doo-Da-Day
You Can Cry On My Shoulder

Music & Me
April 13, 1973
Motown

Side A:
With A Child's Heart
Up Again
All the Things You Are
Happy (from *Lady Sings the Blues*)
Too Young

Side B:
Doggin' Around
Euphoria
Morning Glow
Johnny Raven
Music And Me

Forever, Michael
January 16, 1975
Motown

We're Almost There
Take Me Back
One Day In Your Life
Cinderella Stay Awhile
We've Got Forever
Just A Little Bit of You
You Are There
Dapper-Dan
Dear Michael
I'll Come Home To You

Off the Wall
August 10, 1979
Epic / CBS

Don't Stop 'Til You Get Enough
Rock With You
Working Day And Night
Get On The Floor
Off The Wall
Girlfriend
She's Out Of My Life
I Can't Help It
It's The Falling In Love
Burn This Disco Out

Thriller
November 30, 1982
Epic / CBS

Side one:
Wanna Be Startin' Somethin'
Baby Be Mine
The Girl Is Mine
Thriller

Side two:
Beat It
Billie Jean
Human Nature
P.Y.T. (Pretty Young Thing)
The Lady In My Life

Bad
August 31, 1987
Epic / CBS

Bad
The Way You Make Me Feel
Speed Demon
Liberian Girl
Just Good Friends (with Stevie Wonder)
Another Part Of Me
Man In The Mirror
I Just Can't Stop Loving You (with Siedah Garrett)
Dirty Diana
Smooth Criminal

Dangerous
November 26, 1991
Epic

Jam (ft. Heavy D)
Why You Wanna Trip On Me
In The Closet (ft. Princess Stephanie Of Monaco)
She Drives Me Wild (ft. Wreckx-n-Effect)
Remember The Time
Can't Let Her Get Away
Heal The World
Black Or White (ft. L.T.B.)
Who Is It
Give In To Me (ft. Slash)
Will You Be There (theme from *Free Willy*)
Keep The Faith (ft. Andrae Crouch)
Gone Too Soon
Dangerous

HIStory: Past, Present and Future, Book I
June 16, 1995
Epic / MJJ Productions

Disc one:
Billie Jean
The Way You Make Me Feel
Black Or White
Rock With You
She's Out Of My Life
Bad
I Just Can't Stop Loving You (with Siedah Garrett)
Man In The Mirror
Thriller
Beat It
The Girl Is Mine (with Paul McCartney)
Remember The Time
Don't Stop 'Til You Get Enough

Wanna Be Startin' Somethin'
Heal The World

Disc two:
Scream (with Janet Jackson)
They Don't Care About Us
Stranger In Moscow
This Time Around (ft. Notorious B.I.G.)
Earth Song
D.S. (ft. Slash)
Money
Come Together
You Are Not Alone
Childhood (from *Free Willy 2*)
Tabloid Junkie
2 Bad (ft. Shaquille O'Neal)
HIStory
Little Susie
Smile

Invincible
October 30, 2001
Epic

Unbreakable (ft. The Notorious B.I.G.)
Heartbreaker (ft. Fats)
Invincible (ft. Fats)
Break of Dawn
Heaven Can Wait
You Rock My World
Butterflies
Speechless
2000 Watts
You Are My Life
Privacy
Don't Walk Away
Cry
The Lost Children
Whatever Happens (ft. Carlos Santana)
Threatened

POSTHUMOUS ALBUMS

Michael
December 10 (or 14), 2010
Epic / Sony / MJJ

Hold My Hand (with Akon)
Hollywood Tonight (ft. Taryll Jackson)
Keep Your Head Up
(I Like) The Way You Love Me
Monster (ft. 50 Cent)
Best Of Joy
Breaking News
(I Can't Make It) Another Day (ft. Lenny Kravitz)
Behind The Mask
Much Too Soon

Xscape
May 9, 2014
Epic / Sony / MJJ

Love Never Felt So Good
Chicago
Loving You
A Place With No name
Slave To The Rhythm
Do You Know Where Your Children Are
Blue Gangsta
Xscape
Love Never Felt So Good (Original)
Chicago (Original)
Loving You (Original)
A Place With No Name (Original)
Slave To The Rhythm (Original)
Do You Know Where Your Children Are (Original)
Blue Gangsta (Original)
Xscape (original version)
Love Never Felt So Good (ft. Justin Timberlake)

SINGLES

Got to Be There (1971) – B-side: Maria (You Were The Only One)
Rockin' Robin (1972) – B-side: Love Is Here And Now You're Gone
I Wanna Be Where You Are (1972) – B-side: We've Got A Good Thing Going
Ain't No Sunshine (1972) – B-side: I Wanna Be Where You Are
Ben (1972) – B-side: You Can Cry On My Shoulder
With A Child's Heart (1973) – B-side: Morning Glow
Morning Glow (1973) – B-side: My Girl
Music And Me (1973) – B-side: Johnny Raven
Happy (1973) – B-side: In Our Small Way
We're Almost There (1975) – B-side: Take Me Back
Just A Little Bit Of You (1975) – B-side: Dear Michael
Ease on Down The Road (with Diana Ross) (1978) – B-side: Go On With Your Bad Self
You Can't Win (1979) – B-side: You Can't Win (Pt.2)
A Brand New Day (with Diana Ross & The Wiz Stars) (1979) – B-side: Liberation Ballet – A Brand New Day
Don't Stop 'Til You Get Enough (1979) – B-side: I Can't Help It
Rock With You (1979) – B-side: Get On The Floor (EU) / Working Day And Night (US, UK, Netherlands – both)
Off the Wall (1980) – B-side: Get On The Floor (US) / Working Day and Night (EU)
She's Out Of My Life (1980) – B-side: Push Me Away (UK) / Get On The Floor (US)
Girlfriend (1980) – B-side: Bless His Soul
One Day In Your Life (1981) – B-side: Take Me Back
The Girl Is Mine (with Paul McCartney) (1982) – B-side: Can't Get Outta The Rain
Billie Jean (1983) – B-side: It's The Falling In Love (EU) / Can't Get Outta the Rain (US)
Beat It (1983) – B-side: Get On The Floor (US) / Burn This Disco Out & Don't Stop 'Til You Get Enough (UK)
Wanna Be Startin' Somethin' (1983) – B-side: Rock With You
Human Nature (1983) – B-side: Baby Be Mine
P.Y.T. (Pretty Young Thing) (1983) – B-side: / Working Day And Night (45 RPM version) / This Place Hotel & Thriller Instrumental (Disco single)
Say Say Say (with Paul McCartney) (1983) – B-side: Ode To A Koala Bear
Thriller (1983) – B-side: Things I Do For You
Farewell My Summer Love (1984) – B-side: Call On Me (UK) / Call On Me was also A-Side in the US, and then B-side was Jackson 5 Motown Medley – I Want You Back, The Love You Save, Dancing Machine, ABC, I'll Be There (US)
Girl You're So Together (1984) – B-side: Touch The One You Love
I Just Can't Stop Loving You (with Siedah Garrett) (1987) – B-side: Baby Be Mine
Bad (1987) – B-side: I Can't Help It
The Way You Make Me Feel (1987) – B-side: Instrumental version
Man In The Mirror (1988)
Dirty Diana (1988) – B-side: Bad (Extended Dance Remix)
Another Part Of Me (1988) – B-side: Instrumental version
Smooth Criminal (1988) – B-side:

Instrumental Version
Leave Me Alone (1989) – B-side: Human Nature / Don't Stop 'Til You Get Enough
Liberian Girl (1989) – B-side: Girlfriend (7") / Girlfriend & Get On The Floor (12")
Black Or White (1991) – B-side: Instrumental Version
Remember The Time (1992)
In The Closet (1992)
Jam (1992)
Who Is It (1992)
Heal The World (1992)
Give In To Me (1993)
Will You Be There (1993)
Gone Too Soon (1993)
Scream (with Janet Jackson) (1995) – B-side: Childhood
You Are Not Alone (1995)
Earth Song (1995)
They Don't Care About Us (1996)
Stranger In Moscow (1996)
Blood On The Dance Floor (1997)
HISstory/Ghosts (1997)
You Rock My World (2001)
Cry (2001)
Butterflies (2002)
One More Chance (2003)
The Girl Is Mine 2008 (with will.i.am) (2008)
Wanna Be Startin' Somethin' 2008 (with Akon) (2008)
Hold My Hand (with Akon) (2010)
Hollywood Tonight (2011)
Behind The Mask (2011)
Love Never Felt So Good (with Justin Timberlake) (2014)
A Place With No Name (2014)

TOURS

THE JACKSON 5

First National Tour
May 2, 1970-December 30, 1970
14 shows, US only

Second National Tour
January 2, 1971-August 15, 1971
33 shows, US only

US Tour
December 27, 1971-October 5, 1972
~50 shows, US only

European Tour
November 2, 1972-November 12, 1972
8-10 shows, Europe only

World Tour
March 2, 1973-December 1975
~160 shows, Worldwide

Final Tour
February 13, 1976-February 19, 1976
6 shows, Philippines only

THE JACKSONS

The Jacksons Tour
May 19, 1977-May 24, 1977
Unknown shows, Europe only

Goin' Places Tour
January 22, 1978-May 13, 1978
Unknown shows, US & Europe

Destiny World Tour
January 22, 1979-September 26, 1980
~127 shows, Worldwide

Triumph Tour
July 8, 1981-September 26, 1981
42-44 shows, US only

Victory Tour
July 6, 1984-December 9, 1984
55 Shows, US & Canada

SOLO

Bad
September 12, 1987-January 27, 1989
123 shows, Worldwide

Dangerous
June 27, 1992-November 11, 1993
69-70 shows, Worldwide

HIStory
September 7, 1996-October 15, 1997
82-3 shows, Worldwide

MJ & Friends
June 25, 1999-June 27, 1999
2 shows, South Korea & Germany

This Is It (Cancelled)
July 13, 2009-March 6, 2010
50 shows were scheduled, UK only

FILMOGRAPHY

THE JACKSONS

The Jacksons (1976-7, Bill Davis) – self

MICHAEL JACKSON

The Wiz (1978, Sidney Lumet) – Scarecrow
Wiz on Down the Road (1978, Elliot Geisinger/Ronald Saland) – Scarecrow
Captain EO (1986, Francis Ford Coppola) – Captain EO
Moonwalker (1988, Jerry Kramer) – Michael
The Simpsons (1991, Matt Groening) – Leon Kompowsky
Ghosts (1977, Stan Winston) – Maestro / Mayor / Mayor Ghoul
The Lionhearts (1998) – Voice
Space Channel 5 (1999) – Space Michael
Men in Black 2 (2002, Barry Sonnenfeld) – Agent M
Space Channel 5: Part 2 (2002) – Space Michael
Miss Castaway and the Island Girls (2004, Bryan Michael Stoller) – Agent M.J.

INDEX

CREDITS

The publishers would like to thank Getty Images for their kind permission to reproduce the pictures in this book.

AFP: 60 (bottom), 79, 183; /Afro American Newspapers/Gado: 189; / Carlo Allegri: 122; /ARNAL/PAT/Gamma-Rapho: 114; /Steve Allen/ Liaison: 93; /John Barr/Liaison: 198; /Robyn Beck/AFP: 127 (top), 134; /Dave Benett: 205; /Paul Bergen/Redferns: 206-207; /Bride Lane Library/Popperfoto: 78; /L. Busacca/WireImage: 92; /Peter Carrette Archive: 109; /M. Caulfield/WireImage: 123, 220-221; /CBS Photo Archive: 144-145; /Timothy A. Clary/AFP: 124; /Tim Boxer: 154; /Richard Corkery/NY Daily News Archive: 43, 248; /Lester Cohen/WireImage: 50; /Donna Connor/FilmMagic: 99 (bottom); / Fin Costello/Redferns: 28, 36; /Georges De Keerle: 80-81; /Phil Dent/ Redferns: 1, 3, 115, 196; /DMI/The LIFE Picture Collection: 194; / Kieran Doherty/Redferns: 113; /Echoes/Redferns: 149; /Frank Edwards/Fotos International: 147; /Jonathan Exley/Contour: 95, 112, 121, 126, 130, 136, 203, 209, 210-211, 242-243; /Fotos International: 141; /Andy Freeberg: 158, 162-163; /Ron Galella/WireImage: 60 (top), 76, 87, 96, 171, 185, 192, 193, 202, 230, 231; /Lynn Goldsmith/ Corbis/VCG: 176-177; /Steve Granitz/WireImage: 103; /John Gunion/ Redferns: 199; /Gijsbert Hanekroot/Redferns: 40; /Paul Harris: 117; /John M. Heller: 190; /Dave Hogan: 9, 62, 88-89, 100-101, 108, 110 (top & bottom), 184, 256; /Dave Hogan/Hulton Archive: 182; /Hulton Archive: 155; /Independent News And Media: 91; /Cynthia Johnson/ Liaison: 102; /Kurita Kaku/Gamma-Rapho: 104; /John Kelly/Ebet Roberts/Redferns: 152; /Phil Klein: 244; /Barry King/WireImage: 159, 200; /Jeff Kravitz/FilmMagic: 216 (centre, right), 240-241; /Kypros: 98; /Liaison: 61; /The LIFE Picture Collection: 66, 71, 84 (bottom), 86, 99 (top), 232; /Michel Linssen/Redferns: 239; /Terry Lott/Sony Music Archive: 53, 174; /Kevin Mazur/AEG: 125, 127 (bottom); / Kevin Mazur/WireImage: 10-11, 75, 77 (top), 106-107, 172, 188, 204, 214, 216 (left), 217, 219, 245; /Michael Ochs Archives: 6-7, 14, 16-17, 19, 26, 27, 29, 30, 32, 34-35, 54, 82, 97, 142, 146, 148, 150, 152, 157, 160, 161, 175, 226, 227; /Michael Marks/Michael Ochs Archives: 55; / Jim McCrary/Redferns: 228, 229; /Frank Micelotta/ImageDirect: 94, 116, 238; /Robert R. McElroy: 84 (top); /David McGough/DMI/The LIFE Picture Collection: 64, 233; /Jeffrey Mayer: 65; /Paul Natkin: 191; /John Olson/The LIFE Picture Collection: 15, 24; /Denis O'Regan: 58-59; /Gilles Petard/Redferns: 18; /Michael Putland: 42, 70; /RB/ Redferns: 23, 31; /David Redfern/Redferns: 37; /Bob Riha Jr: 169; / Ebet Roberts/Redferns: 44, 45, 46-47, 49, 52, 56-57, 63, 187; /John Roca/NY Daily News Archive: 72, 195; /Sankei Archive: 77 (bottom), 128; /Lawrence Schiller/Polaris Communications: 20-21; /Bob Scott/ Liaison: 74; /Tom Sheehan/Sony Music Archive: 33; /Ed Souza: 131; / Gus Stewart/Redferns: 39; /Peter Still/Redferns: 167; /Diana Walker/ Liaison: 83; /Chris Walter/WireImage: 51, 85, 165, 166, 180-181; /Phil Walter: 212-213; /Julian Wasser/Liaison: 67; /Angela Weiss: 132-133; /Kimberly White: 129; /Steven Paul Whitsitt/Contour: 111, 118-119, 236; /Kevin Winter: 90; /Kevin Winter/Billboard Awards 2014: 135; /Rafael Wollmann/Gamma-Rapho: 235; /Vinnie Zuffante/Hulton Archive: 68-69

The following photographs were supplied by REX/Shutterstock: 168-169, 178 (Eugene Adebari) & 179 (SIPA)

Every effort has been made to acknowledge correctly and contact the source and/or copyright holder of each picture and Carlton Publishing Group apologises for any unintentional errors or omissions that will be corrected in future editions of this book.

Above Still at the top of his game, a defiant Michael stares out at a New York City crowd in 1997.